Bibliography
of
the British Technology Index

Compiled by
Keiichi Kawamura, PhD

Jusonbo Co. Ltd.
Tokyo

Bibliography of the British Technology Index
Compiled by Keiichi Kawamura

This bibliography lists about 320 references to BTI ranging from 1958 to the present. Eight languages are concerned with the bibliography: English, Finnish, French, German, Hungarian, Japanese, Spanish and Swedish. Every item has an English abstract or annotation. Items are arranged in systematic order, and cross-references among related items as well as author and language indexes complement the systematic arrangement. A title list of E.J. Coates' BTI-related works arranged in chronological order is appended.

Published by Jusonbo Co. Ltd.
5-11-7 Koishikawa, Bunkyo-ku, Tokyo 112-0002, Japan
Tel: +81 (0)3 3868 7321
Fax: +81 (0)3 6801 5202
http://www.jusonbo.co.jp

ISBN978-4-88367-250-9

Copyright © 2015 Keiichi Kawamura. All rights reserved.

No part of this publication may be reproduced or transmitted in any form or by any means, electronic or mechanical, including photocopying, recording, or any information storage and retrieval system, without prior written permission from the publisher.

Cover: Reproduced from the *British Technology Index. Annual volume 1976*, by courtesy of CILIP, London.

Typeset and design by BERTH Office, Japan.
Printed and bound in Japan by Kurashiki Printing Co., Ltd.

Undoubtedly the most important contribution to the theory of alphabetical subject headings for many years is the work of E.J. Coates. ... He has also had the challenge of putting his ideas into practice on a large scale in the *British Technology Index*, of which he has been editor since its inception – an opportunity of a kind which rarely presents itself to the theorist.   (A.C. Foskett, 1977)

The essential difference between relational and facet analysis is that in the latter case it is the terms in a syntactic string which are themselves considered, while in the former case one considers the linkages between the terms.   (E.J. Coates, 1974)

The staff are encouraged to deal with subject heading problems in classificatory terms.
                                                                                                                          (E.J. Coates, 1962)

I was certainly not the only technical librarian who must have provided a much less satisfactory service but for BTI.   (K.G.B. Bakewell, 1982)

I hope therefore that the BTI will be supported by British special librarians not only on account of the various ways in which it may be immediately helpful, but also because it is a step in the right direction – towards wider bibliographical control, which we all desire to see extended to technical literature originating in all parts of the world.   (E.J. Coates, 1962)

Preface and Acknowledgements

Do you know the *British Technology Index* or BTI? I would like to ask anyone who is concerned with alphabetical subject indexing of information.

BTI was commenced by the Library Association (LA), London, in February 1962. It was a monthly and annual subject guide to articles in about 400 British technical journals. There had been two commercial efforts to provide a technical indexing service in the United Kingdom (UK) in the 1950s, both of which had failed. BTI was a venture of the LA and was full of drama. As of 1976 A.C. Foskett described BTI as follows:

"*British Technology Index* was launched in 1962, and immediately set out to provide a detailed indexing service for current scanning, in which production time was kept to a minimum. It has never had a large staff, yet it has continued to work to a very tight schedule while maintaining a high standard of indexing. The theories involved have stood up to the searching test of mechanisation and come through with flying colours. ... The subject headings used have been criticised, particularly in the early years, but perhaps the best answer to that is the fact that BTI has, despite unfavourable omens and without access to substantial resources, established itself as a reference tool of international standing. The effectiveness of the indexing system has been the basis of this success."

BTI was held in high repute among the user community. However, the drama still continued. The editor, E.J. Coates, was appointed in September 1974 as one of the three-man panel of the FID/BSO (Broad System of Ordering) in the UNISIST programme and he later became Rapporteur of the FID/BSO Panel. He resigned the editorship of BTI in the spring of 1977, and several events affecting BTI followed in succession. The final and unexpected event was the change of title, which was accompanied by a somewhat different format. BTI was changed to CTI (Current Technology Index) in 1981, and the title was changed again to ANTE (Abstracts in New Technologies and Engineering) in 1997.

The indexing system of BTI had a sound theoretical basis. Prior to the commencement of BTI, Coates' main book "*Subject catalogues: headings and structure*" was published by the LA in 1960. In this book he summarized succinctly previous approaches to alphabetical subject cataloguing, such as those of Cutter, Kaiser, Ranganathan and Farradane, and put forward his own theory. Two years later he took an opportunity to put his theory into practice in BTI. Coates argued that all forms of subject catalogue have a two-fold objective: identifying a specific subject and browsing related subjects. A feature of BTI was the 'block structure' under the same main subject heading, while keeping strictly alphabetical form. This was realized by creating logically articulated subject headings based on relationships between concepts and by a chain procedure for generating cross-references from these subject headings.

As one of the original members of the Classification Research Group (CRG) in London, Coates was influenced by Ranganathan. He inherited Ranganathan's thought of 'the unity of subject indication' which embraces all kinds of classification and subject indexing. He was convinced that alphabetical subject indexing systems possess, or should possess, some form of classificatory correlation. Coates also advanced relational analysis, which was first propounded by Farradane, in the light of classification. This is definitely worth studying.

BTI introduced new techniques which differed from those traditionally used. Societies of professional indexers regarded BTI as 'an indexing masterpiece' in the field of science and technology, and Coates was called 'the genius of subject index.' His main book was reissued by the same publisher in 1988 at an interval of 28 years. I think that it is time to reappraise BTI as a global standard. The bibliography is compiled for this purpose.

Acknowledgement is due to Dr. Leonard Will, of Willpower Information, Enfield, UK, for helping with some references and for reviewing the preface and introduction. I am grateful to Prof. Naoki Takubo, of Kindai University, Osaka, Japan, for his valuable counsel and encouragement. I should like to thank those who supplied abstracts of the non-English literature: Prof. Agnes Hajdu Barat, of the University of Szeged, Hungary; Mrs. Karin Ekstrom, of the library of the University of Boras, Sweden; Ms. Ika Mantani, of Dokkyo University and Mr. Akira Ueda, Japan. I thank Ms. Hiromi Okada, a librarian at Dokkyo Medical University, for technical assistance. I wish to express my gratitude to Mr. Eiichi Otsuka, president of Jusonbo Co. Ltd., for undertaking to publish the work.

With regard to the kind permission to reproduce materials from copyrighted publications, special thanks are due to: the Chartered Institute of Library and Information Professionals (CILIP), London, UK, who inherited the copyrights to the former Library Association's publications, such as *Annual report of the Council of the Association, Library Association Record, Liaison, Library Science Abstracts* (LSA), and so on; ProQuest, Ann Arbor, Michigan, USA, who hold the copyright to *Library and Information Science Abstracts* (LISA); and the editor of *The Indexer* which is an organ of the Society of Indexers, Sheffield, UK, for a number of articles that appeared in the journal.

Finally I wish to dedicate the work to my wife, Eriko Kawamura, who has supported me all these many years until her passing on the 20th of November, 2014.

Keiichi Kawamura
18th June 2015

Table of Contents

Preface and acknowledgements 5

Introduction 9

Systematic arrangement 11

  00 "Subject catalogues: headings and structure" 12

    00.10 Bibliographic information on the original edition, reprints and reissue, 00.20 Summary and recommendations, 00.30 Partial reprints in USA, 00.40 Reviews of the original edition published in 1960, 00.50 Reviews of the reissue published in 1988, 00.60 References made to Coates' theory of subject catalogues

  10 Prenatal stage and early years of BTI 27

    10.10 Prospects for a new subject index to British technical journals, 10.20 Scepticism and controversy, 10.30 Reviews of monthly issue, 10.40 Reviews of annual volumes

  20 Aspects of BTI 43

    20.10 General description, 20.20 Coverage, 20.30 Currency (Time-lag), 20.40 Promotion and subscription rates, 20.50 Number of subscriptions, 20.60 Change of size, 20.70 Use of magnetic tape, 20.80 Microfiche form, 20.90 Others

  30 Indexing system 55

    30.10 General description, 30.20 Relational analysis and citation order, 30.30 Handling of compound terms, 30.40 Vocabulary control, 30.50 Chain procedure for generating cross-references from subject headings, 30.60 References made to BTI with other systems

  40 Computerization 69

    40.10 Overview, 40.20 Announcements and news items, 40.30 Reports by the project director and the programmer, 40.40 Hardware and software

  50 User-oriented education and training 84

    50.10 Discussion meetings, lectures and workshops on BTI indexing system, 50.20 Instruction in use of bibliographic tools including BTI

  60 User study and laboratory evaluation 88

    60.10 Editor's opinion on index evaluation, 60.20 INSPEC, 60.30 EPSILON

  70 Events following the resignation of the first editor 93

  80 Applications of BTI system including trials and discussions 99

    80.10 CTI, 80.20 ASSIA, 80.30 NRPRA, 80.40 Metal Box Ltd., 80.50 SEA project, 80.60 STIR project, 80.70 Decentralized indexing in a centralized system using classification, 80.80 Recommendation for the index form in standards

  90 References made to BTI in connection with Ranganathan and CRG 109

Author index 115

Language index 121

Appendix: Title list of Coates' BTI-related works arranged in chronological order 123

7

Introduction

Outline

This bibliography lists about 320 references to BTI ranging from 1958 to the present. The largest and most important section of the bibliography is a single sequence of entries arranged in systematic order. Every item has an English abstract or annotation.

Coverage and selection

The bibliography aims at comprehensiveness as far as possible. It covers: (1) journal articles, (2) conference papers, (3) reports, (4) monograph chapters or sections, (5) seminar works, (6) announcements, (7) news items, (8) letters, (9) book reviews, and so on. No attempt has been made to list items that are not primarily concerned with BTI. However, some items on other topics have been included if they are thought to provide supplementary information on BTI, either relating to features of the system which are considered noteworthy or if they deal with new aspects of the system.

Arrangement

Schedules for the systematic arrangement of items constitute a large part of the table of contents. The schedules consist of 10 main classes. In the first class (00) items dealing with Coates' main book "*Subject catalogues: headings and structure*" are collected. They give information on the original edition, reprints and reissue of the book, and on reviews of these. In the remaining classes (10 to 90) BTI publications and related items are listed. The purpose of systematic arrangement is to group related materials. Therefore, for instance, book reviews are listed with the publication that they discuss and the item number of each book review is accompanied by that of the publication in brackets.

Entries

Each entry consists of: (1) item number, (2) bibliographic description, and (3) abstract or annotation. In the case of journal articles, which constitute the majority of items included, the following bibliographic elements are given in order: (1) original English title or English translation of title in boldface, (2) author(s) if any, (3) journal title in italics together with an ISSN in brackets, (4) volume number, (5) issue or part number in brackets, (6) month or season, (7) year of publication, and (8) inclusive pagination. Titles in English are given as they appear in the literature. Titles in other European languages using the Roman alphabet are given in both translated and original forms. Other titles using non-Roman-alphabet are given in translated forms only, but where titles using non-Roman-alphabets are the results of translation from English, these are given in both transliterated and original English forms. Author names are also given as they appear in the literature. As a matter of convenience all diacritical marks are omitted in this bibliography.

Abstracts

Abstracts used in entries are taken from various sources: (1) original abstracts, (2) abstracts supplied by the compiler's colleagues for a book chapter in German and book reviews in Hungarian, Spanish and Swedish, and (3) abstracts of secondary information services. Below is a list of secondary information services in which abstracts are looked up.

LSA – *Library Science Abstracts*, 1950-68 (UK)
LISA – *Library and Information Science Abstracts*, 1969-present (UK)
DA – *Documentation Abstracts*, 1966-68 (USA)
ISA – *Information Science Abstracts*, 1969-2002 (USA)
AJI – *Abstract Journal. Informatics*, 1970-76 (USSR)
IA – *Informatics Abstracts*, 1977-91 (USSR)

The abstract chosen for an entry depends upon the judgement of the compiler. The source is indicated in brackets at the end of abstract. Where an abstract or annotation was written by the compiler, his initials (KK) are indicated in brackets.

Indexes

The bibliography provides indexes to authors and to languages of texts written in one of the seven non-English languages which are present. Author names in the index are in most cases given in more detail than in the systematic arrangement. Both indexes refer to item numbers.

Appendix

A title list of Coates' BTI-related works arranged in chronological order is appended at the end of the bibliography.

Omissions

Though this bibliography aims at comprehensiveness, there may be serious omissions. Information from readers will be appreciated. The address of the compiler is as follows: Keiichi Kawamura, 5-30-5 Midori, Shimotsuke-shi, Tochigi 329-0433, Japan (e-mail: kawamura.bso@gmail.com).

Systematic Arrangement

00 "SUBJECT CATALOGUES: HEADINGS AND STRUCTURE"

00.10 Bibliographic information on the original edition, reprints and reissue

#1   **Subject catalogues: headings and structure** / E.J. Coates – London, Library Association, 1960, 186p. Reprinted in 1963 and 1969, 186p. Reissued with new preface in 1988, 186p. (ISBN 0-85365-678-9). For preface to 1988 reissue, see #312.

The original edition consists of 14 chapters: (I) Terminology; (II) Subject recording and recovery; (III) The two-fold objective; (IV) Towards systematisation; (V) Subject heading theory after Cutter; (VI) Significance and term relationship in compound headings; (VII) The dictionary catalogue since Cutter; (VIII) The contribution of classification; (IX) Chain procedure for subject indexes to classified catalogues; (X) Chain procedure applied to the Decimal Classification; (XI) Chain procedure and the alphabetico-specific catalogue; (XII) Group arrangement in the subject index; (XIII) Use and search strategy; and (XIV) The role of conventional classification schemes. The move of reprints in paperback form was to make the book more available to students. The book had been out of print since the middle of the 1970s. The original edition was reissued with the author's new preface in hardcover form by the same publisher in 1988. "Preface to 1988 reissue" reviewed the aims and motivation of writing the book and the impact of mechanization on subject cataloguing since 1960. (KK)

00.20 Summary and recommendations

#2(#1)   **[Summary of] Subject catalogues: headings and structure** – *Unesco Bulletin for Libraries* (ISSN 0041-5243), 14(4)July-August 1960, p.179.

Little progress has been made in the last half-century towards the achievement of a systematic working rationale in subject cataloguing. This work relates the structural features of the alphabetical and classified forms to each other and to the various types of questions put by inquirers. The contributions of Cutter, Kaiser, and Ranganathan [and Farradane] to alphabetical subject cataloguing are considered. Subject indexes to classification schemes, and to two main varieties of classified catalogues are examined and Ranganathan's chain procedure is outlined. A further chapter discusses the role of classification and chain procedure in alphabetical subject and dictionary cataloguing. Finally, an attempt is made to lay down the elements of search strategy for dealing with inquiries addressed to subject catalogues. (Original abstract)

#3(#1)   **[Recommendation of] Subject catalogues: headings and structure** / A.C. Foskett – In his: *The subject approach to information* – London, Clive Bingley, 1969, p.16 and 53.

One of the few worthwhile books on the alphabetical approach. Not easy, but essential reading. ... The first six chapters are essential reading. Students should also study carefully at least one of the annual volumes of *British technology index*, to see how Coates' principles are applied in practice. (Excerpt from original text)

#4 (#1) [Recommendation of] Subject catalogues: headings and structure / Paul S. Dunkin – In his: *Cataloging U.S.A.* – Chicago, American Library Association, 1969, p.xx.

Although basically British in attitude, this book is of considerable value for its rather logical study of Cutter, its account of what has happened to subject headings since Cutter, and its suggested solutions. (Excerpt from original text)

00.30 Partial reprints in USA

#5 (#1) [Chapter VI] Significance and term relationship in compound headings / E.J. Coates – Reprinted in: *Theory of subject analysis: a source book* / ed. Lois Mai Chan, Phyllis A. Richmond and Elaine Svenonius – Littleton, CO, Libraries Unlimited, 1985, p.181-195. (ISBN 0-87287-489-3).

This selection from Coates' *Subject catalogues: headings and structure* proposes the concept "term significance," the word that evokes the clearest mental image used as criterion for determining the entry element in a compound heading. A relationship table that shows how compound subjects are to be classified is given. The problem of classifying phrases and names of localities in headings are also discussed. Coates theory was put into practice in compiling the *British Technology Index* from 1961 [sic] to 1977 [sic]. (ISA 85-11726)

#6 (#1) Library of Congress practice / Eric James Coates – Reprinted in: *Improving LCSH for use in online catalogs: exercises for self-help with a selection of background readings* / Pauline A. Cochrane – Littleton, CO, Libraries Unlimited, 1986, p.140-147. (ISBN 0-87287-484-2).

This part is a section of Chapter VII: The dictionary catalogue since Cutter. Describes that the Library of Congress list has modeled broadly on the basis provided by Cutter, but with a continuous series of modifications to meet new circumstances. Little or no attempt has been made to keep theory abreast of the developing practice. Stresses that there is a relationship between the system of connective references and the manner in which compound subjects are handled. Points out that underlying ambiguities in both lurks the hesitancy in applying the principle of specific subject entry, which results in confusing inconsistencies. Says that there seem to be two distinct and separate layers of relational references in the LC list, and that a connective reference system based on classification alone does not suffice for a dictionary catalogue. The part had been preceded by Coates' review article entitled "Alphabetical subject catalogues", *Journal of Documentation* (ISSN 0022-0418), 9(1) March 1953, p.58-63. (KK)

00.40 Reviews of the original edition published in1960

#7(#1)   [Review of] Subject catalogues: headings and structure / S.J. Butcher – *Assistant Librarian* (ISSN 0004-5152), 53(7)July 1960, p.149-151.

Coates is wise enough to recognize that any attempt to evaluate one form of subject catalogue against the other is fruitless and raises issues of subordinate importance. After describing and evaluating the contributions of Cutter, Kaiser, Ranganathan and Farradane to the theory of subject work, Coates examines the value of classification as a determinant of component order. From here, a large proportion of the work is devoted to an outline of Ranganathan's chain procedure. Of particular interest is the chapter dealing with the application of the method to DDC. Coates reveals that one important reason for the adoption of chain indexing by BNB was the need for exceptional speed of decision in subject indexing. He admits the common difficulty of the incomplete modulation of terms in DDC. It is obvious that chain indexing cannot be better than the scheme to which it is applied. This is not an easy book to read, but the author has achieved no means success in describing and discussing technical aspects of subject cataloguing. This is really a book for the specialist and not a primer for the students. (KK)

#8(#1)   [Review of] Subject catalogues: headings and structure / D.J. Foskett – *Library Association Record* (ISSN 0024-2195), 62(6)June 1960, p.201-202.

The book is reviewed, together with John Metcalfe's *Subject classifying and indexing of libraries and literature* (1950). Says that Coates made no resounding claims in contrast with Metcalfe. But the book is a *tour de force*. Like Metcalfe, Coates starts with a statement of objectives, and follows this with a historical account of the development of systematic structure in cataloguing. The reviewer likes the discussions of the comparative structure of three main forms of catalogue and of the different types of relationship between terms and how they should be represented in a heading, both of which are summarized in a tabular form. Concludes that Coates' main theme is that cataloguers and classifiers need a systematic technique for subject analysis. In this respect faceted classification and chain indexing offer such a technique, even though they are not entirely successful with the existing general classification schemes, and there is plenty of evidence to show that this is actually the most promising development in this field for many years. (KK)

#9(#1)   [Review of] Subject catalogues: headings and structure / K.C. Harrison – *Library World* (ISSN 0024-2616), 61(719)May 1960, p.237.

Those who have read the occasional articles and know the other work of Eric Coates are convinced that what he writes will be competent. This will be said of this work. He devotes the first chapter to terminology, but he has not overduly created new terms or new meanings for old ones. The work is comprehensive and practical, and to the person who finds happiness in cataloguing, this is a work of great interest. There are selective references and notes at the chapter ends and a competent index. It makes a useful companion to B.C. Vickery's *Classification and indexing in science*. (KK)

#10(#1) **[Review of] Subject catalogues: headings and structure** / Marjorie Plant – *Journal of Documentation* (ISSN 0022-0418), 16(3)September 1960, p.151-152.

This work has provided a survey of the whole problem of subject catalogues and their structure. Coates' treatment of the contributions of Cutter, Kaiser, Ranganathan to alphabetical subject catalogues and of the various types of subject index to classification schemes and classified catalogues is most satisfactory which has appeared in a single book. It includes a lucid explanation of chain procedure and of its application to BNB with authority. Criticizes Coates for thinking in terms of the library and information staff and not the ultimate user, as undertaking the search in the catalogue. The reviewer believes that it causes serious problem when a chain index is searched by a user. (KK)

#11(#1) **[Review of] Subject catalogues: headings and structure** / Henry A. Sharp – *Library Review* (ISSN 0024-2535), (134)Summer 1960, p.424.

This is a good and useful book for students and for practicing cataloguers, but one is rather a cleft stick about the book. While the reviewer has the greatest admiration for the work of BNB, he believes that one cannot agree to an advocacy of the chain indexing. Nevertheless, the three chapters on it will be useful for students. Coates is in charge of the subject side of BNB, and sets out to relate "the structural features of the alphabetical and classified to each other, and to the various types of question put by enquirers." Emphasizes that the problem of chain indexing must not be entirely due to BNB but to Ranganathan. Altogether the book is a valuable contribution to cataloguing literature, but points out that the well-compiled index includes many strange terms that the reviewer had never heard. (KK)

#12(#1) **[Review of] Subject catalogues: headings and structure** / Kenneth W. Soderland – *Library Quarterly* (ISSN 0024-2519), 31(1)January 1961, p.120-121.

One of the main concerns of the book is the merits of an alphabetical versus a classified subject catalogue. He sums up that classification is the only tool which reveals the full variety of names under which a single concept may be discussed. The problem of compound subject headings is another matter of great concern to him. He discusses the different subject heading theories of Kaiser, Ranganathan and Farradane and how they differ from Cutter's. The third matter in this book is Ranganathan's chain procedure for subject indexes. A chain is a hierarchy of terms in a classification scheme. He maintains that this procedure is more economical, more readily produced mechanically, and more effective than are other means of devising subject indexes and cross-references. This book is well written, logical, and profusely illustrated with examples and tables for ease of understanding, and should be read by every student of advanced cataloguing. (KK)

#13(#1)   **[Review of] Subject catalogues: headings and structure** / J.L. Thornton – *Indexer* (ISSN 0019-4131), 2(2)Autumn 1960, p.72.

Subject cataloguing is of primary importance in librarianship, but it has been neglected except for the publication of a few articles in periodicals. Coates' long experience with the *British National Bibliography* and his up-to-date approach to the problems of cataloguing and classification ensured that the product of his pen would be both authentic and comprehensive. This book is a reliable guide to subject cataloguing, and can be recommended to cataloguers and to students possessing background knowledge of the subject. Indexers can benefit considerably from reading this book. Those who are interested in chain indexing will be particularly fascinated by the three chapters: "Chain procedure for subject indexes to classified catalogues," "Chain procedure applied to the Decimal Classification," and "Chain procedure and the alphabetico-specific catalogue." References for further study are provided at the end of each chapter, and a necessary introduction to the terminology is given in Chapter I. This is a worthy addition to the Library Association's list of publications, and will be of practical value as a guide to subject cataloguing. (KK)

#14(#1)   **Dual approach to subject analysis [Review of] Subject catalogues: headings and structure** / Sarah K. Vann – *Library Journal* (ISSN 0000-0027), 85(12)June 1960, p.2406-2407.

This study may be regarded as a continuation of the views expressed by B.I. Palmer and A.J. Wells in *The fundamentals of library classification* (1951). It is a provocative polemic of the Ranganathanite concept of chain procedure applied to subject cataloguing. The essence of the content is its appraisal of the structural features of the alphabetico-specific and the alphabetico-classed subject catalogues. Coates says that there has been no intellectual successor to Cutter, who was the primary rationalizer of alphabetico-specific subject cataloguing. Makes an evaluation of the contributions of Kaiser, Ranganathan and Farradane. In the Ranganathanite school, the inadequacy of the LC subject headings lies in their not stemming from a classificatory background. While not so comprehensive as John Metcalfe's *Subject classifying and indexing of libraries and literature* (1959), the book provides an intelligible review of the dual approach to subject analysis to which it limits itself. (KK)

#15(#1)   **[Review of] Subject catalogues: headings and structure** [Review in French] / Eric de Grolier – *Bulletin des Bibliotheques de France* (ISSN 0006-2006), 6(5)Mai 1961, p.232-233.

Says that Mr. Coates, who is one of the editorial staff of the *British National Bibliography*, gives us an interesting book. The book begins with a brief introduction to terminology where it distinguishes three types of subject catalogue: alphabetico-specific, systematic and alphabetico-systematic (mixed). He summarizes the ideas of Cutter, and makes a historical study of "Subject heading theory after Cutter," which summarizes the contributions of Kaiser, Ranganathan and Farradane. Chapter VI is devoted to analysis of relations between terms composing headings. As a result there is a "Relationship table" consisting of 20 types of relations. The next chapter entitled "The dictionary catalogue since Cutter" deals with the American practice, especially that of the Library of Congress. The hinge of the book is Chapter VIII entitled "The contribution of classification." Next three are devoted to the illustration of 'chain procedure.' Coates is a fervent adept at the method, but the Aslib-Cranfield Research Project resulted in negative conclusion. In the next chapter, dealing with the formation of groups in the subject index, Coates presents a method to identify the 'fundamental class' of each subject. The book ends with a chapter on the 'search strategy' and two-page remarks on the relationship between classification and natural language. (KK)

#16(#1) **[Review of] Subject catalogues: headings and structure** [Review in Hungarian] / Zsofia Nemeth – *Magyar Konyvszemle* (ISSN 0025-0171), 77(3)Augusztus 1961, p.342-343.

The reviewer summarises the scholarly work of Coates, particularly his long practical experience with BNB. Coates emphasizes fifty years' omission in the USA where librarians have neglected to study theoretical problems of subject catalogues. Cites Coates' remark on the decision of the Library of Congress about subjects that they make peremptory and inconsequent selections, which do not lead to a unitary system. While the reviewer has admiration for the work of BNB, thinks that one cannot agree to an advocacy of chain indexing. Following a description and evaluation of the contributions of Cutter, Kaiser, Ranganathan and Farradane to the theory of subject headings, Coates examines the value of classification as a determinant of component order. He analyses possibilities of the selection of subjects and accentuates disadvantages of phrase headings. He describes problem of subjects with complexity. In the last part he attempts to determine the retrieval strategy in subject catalogues. He illustrates his ideas with many practical examples. The book would be a good and useful tool for students and for practising cataloguers. (Agnes Hajdu Barat)

#17(#1) **[Review of] Subject catalogues: headings and structure** [Review in Swedish] / Lars Tynell – *Biblioteksbladet* (ISSN 0006-1867), 46(2)Februari 1961, p.117.

The term "subject catalogue," as it is used in this book, covers in the Swedish library parlance the systematic catalogue, the alphabetical subject catalogue and the subject bibliography. The analyses, which the author gives of these types of catalogue structure, are highly theoretically oriented and are built on exceedingly extensive studies in the English language literature. Some readers with focus on practical catalogue issues would perhaps secretly wish that the author had a little less read in, for example, Mr Ranganathan's writings. Ranganathan's subtle theories on classification of such subject as "a model of the tower of a castle from Tudor times" belong in spaces, where we ordinary workers in the vineyard rarely have reason to raise. Mr Coates performs the feat to discuss an example of this in two printed pages without the slightest nod to its readers. (Karin Ekstrom)

00.50 Reviews of the reissue published in 1988

#18(#1)   Dated but not outdated [Review of] Subject catalogues: headings and structure / Keith V. Trickey – *Library Association Record* (ISSN 0024-2195), 90(12) December 1988, p.734.

  This is a re-issue of the 1960 classic with a new preface by the author. The reason why a complete revision or a new edition is not attempted can be found in the author's comment at the close of the book, i.e. it is the middle country between classification and natural language which has been reconnoitered in this book. Any attempt to re-write the book would destroy the strength of the author's case. With great precision and insight, Coates guides us through a 'state of the art' review (as of 1960) of subject analysis for headings systems: problems with LCSH, inconsistency in hierarchy in DDC (16th ed.) as a basis for chain indexing, Ranganathan's CC and chain procedure. The rigour of chapter VI 'Significance and term relationship in compound headings' still evoked the same fear as when first encountered. Though dated, the book is worth reading for the acuity of the author's analysis based on a detailed knowledge of practice. The feature which dates the work is the natural obsession with entry word, and concept order within heading. But searching in the machine environment removes this concern. The 'Preface to 1988 reissue' manages to cover a brief review of the vast array of current concerns in language-based subject access. Hopes that this precision and perception can be absorbed by the reader and thus language-based subject access systems improved. (KK)

#19(#1)   [Review of] Subject catalogues: headings and structure / Elaine Svenonius – *Information Processing & Management* (ISSN 0306-4573), 26(1) 1990, p.187-188. See also #22.

  More than a quarter of a century has passed since the work under review was written. Cautions that any state-of-the-art description in the work, such as that of the dictionary catalog, is not only of limited historical interest but also someone's giving an idea, i.e. an idea being classified catalog complemented by a chain index. Points out that it is a misleading of Cutter to suppose a definition of 'specificity' in terms of 'coextensivity,' and that Coates does not doubt for a moment that one can precisely state the subject of a document. In this connection he has been challenged by Patrick Wilson. Argues that the development of the dictionary catalog in the United States was occasioned by a distrust of European classified catalog, which was designed for a scholar, not the common man, and was inadequate for the finding function. It is hoped that there may yet come a useful resolution perhaps with the help of automation and a higher flight of theory. In this respect stresses that Coates' thinking about 'compound terms' and 'chain indexing' are worth studying today. Concludes that Coates not only introduced a British perspective to Ranganathan's views on these matters, but also extended the underlying theory. (KK)

#20(#1) **[Review of] Subject catalogues: headings and structure** / Neville Wood – *Library Review* (ISSN 0024-2535), 39(1)1990, p.54.

The book is reissued almost three decades since its first publication, with a most perceptive preface by its author. The same period has seen developments in author and title cataloguing with the appearance of two editions and a revision of Anglo-American Cataloguing Rules and the growing adoption of online public access catalogues (OPACs). The book outlines the path of what Coates calls "the mainstream subject indication intuitive craft" and treats the contributions of Cutter, Kaiser, Ranganthan and Farradane as well as providing a helpful introductory chapter on essential terminology. The book examines larger themes which includes contrasting classified and dictionary catalogues and the contribution of classification. Coates propounds "Two-fold objective," which means that all subject catalogues, irrespective of their form, must enable firstly the retrieval of a given subject and secondly make known the existence of allied subjects. This founding concept is as valid – perhaps even more valid – in the light of the discernible weakness to date of the subject retrieval capacity of OPACs. For the student of information retrieval this is an essential text because it provides a necessary bedrock on which understanding rather than mere acquaintance with the subject is built. (KK)

00.60 References made to Coates' theory of subject catalogues

See also class 90 References made to BTI in connection with Ranganathan and CRG.

#21 **The alphabetical subject catalogue** / John R. Sharp – In his: *Some fundamentals of information retrieval* – London, Andre Deutsch, 1965, p.48-67 (esp. p.51-58). (SBN 233-95712-X).

Recognizes that a very significant event in recent years was the appearance of the book "*Subject catalogues*" by E.J. Coates. He has tried to substitute a system of determining component order in complex headings by considering how things, materials, actions, etc. are related in subject statements and formulating rules. He put these ideas into practice as the editor of the *British Technology Index*. Discusses problems of subject headings in detail from the stand point of both the indexer and the searcher. Concludes that Coates' rules as a whole may prove to be quite acceptable, but what seems doubtful is whether a really significant proportion of all the possible problems has really been catered for. (KK)

#22   **Subject and the sense of position** / Patrick Wilson – In his: *Two kinds of power: an essay on bibliographic control* – Berkeley, University of California Press, 1968, p.69-72. Reprinted in 1978, p.69-72. (University of California publications in librarianship, 5) (ISBN 0-52003-515-1). See also #19.

Says that it is difficult enough to discover a man's purposes by examining the results of his activity, and that the difficulties must be much greater than ordinary in the case of these most complex products of human effort, i.e. writings. Things are what they are, i.e. our descriptions may be vague and imprecise and indefinite, but there can be no vagueness or indefiniteness about things themselves. Now we have an inclination to say that what is true of things must be true of writings "about" things. It is this inclination that we must be resisted. In this connection Coates is challenged as follows: (1) If he found it incredible that writings have single subjects, he would not have given such a definition of an "alphabetical subject catalogue" as one in which the headings "state precisely the subject of each document, chapter, section, paragraph, or the literary unit chosen as the basis for indexing." (2) He describes the basic operation of subject cataloguing as being essentially "summarization," which is "the abstraction of the overall idea embodied in the subject content of a given unit", and as "the art of reducing to a single idea the content of a piece of literature." But subject headings are not themselves summaries of writings; and if they represent "overall concepts covered" or "overall ideas embodied" in the writings, it is not necessary by summarization of writings that appropriate subject headings are selected. (3) He does not try to say how that reduction art is to be taught, nor does he suggest ways of evaluating the products of the art. Concludes that perhaps he thinks these the sort of things which every intelligent person already knows. (KK)

#23   **Citation order: subject indexing** / Antony Croghan – *Catalogue & Index* (ISSN 0008-7629), (19)July 1970, p.4-5.

Abridgement of a paper at the Spring Seminar, "Subject to information," Aberystwyth, 1970. Considers the work of Cutter, Kaiser, Haykin, Ranganathan (and his influence on the *British National Bibliography*), and Coates (including the subject arrangement in *British Technology Index*). Discusses the Classification Research Group's new General Classification and its influence on BNB's PRECIS project. Investigation into verbal forms used by BTI and PRECIS in comparison with natural language forms is needed. There may be no citation order based solely on language structure that would work but so far it has not been tried. (LISA 70/2027)

#24   **The subject approach: recent developments in indexing** / A.C. Foskett – *Journal of Librarianship* (ISSN 0022-2232), 4(4)October 1972, p.240-252.

Edited version of a paper at the Association of Assistant Librarians Course, 'Cataloguing and indexing: recent developments,' Folkestone, March 1972. Sections cover the historical background; shelf arrangement; the complexity explosion; notational complexity; user unwillingness to tolerate complex notation; classification by primary facet only; and alphabetical headings, exemplified the *British Technology Index*. The complexity explosion has led to ever-increasing difficulties in subject specification, especially in the use of notation. The British National Bibliography's use of DDC18 and PRECIS forms a substantial contribution to the solution of these difficulties, particularly in view of the increased pressure for standardisation arising from computers. (LISA 72/2609)

#25 **Coates [and] Chain procedure** / A.C. Foskett – In his: *The subject approach to information* – London, Clive Bingley, 1969, p.46-53. (SBN 85157-077-1).

Two continuous sections included in Chapter 4: Alphabetical arrangement (p.32-53). Describes that undoubtedly the most important contribution to the theory of alphabetical subject headings for many years is the work of E.J. Coates. In his book, *Subject catalogues*, Coates has summarized succinctly the previous approaches, and put forward his own theories as to the correct formulation of specific subject headings. He begins his study of order in composite headings by trying to establish the reason for Kaiser's selection of Concrete rather than Process as the entry point. Coates uses the terminology Thing-Action and develops his ideas much further based on his principle of 'significance order.' From here he can again move forward to incorporate Material and Part, which gives us Thing-Part-Material-Action formula. Coates also shows how other variants can be built up by following the same principle. He suggests modified form of chain procedure which was originally devised by Ranganathan. Coates has also had the challenge of putting his ideas into practice in the *British Technology Index*, of which he has been editor since its inception – an opportunity of a kind which rarely presents itself to the theorist. (KK)

#26 **Coates [and] Chain procedure** / A.C. Foskett – In his: *The subject approach to information,* 2nd ed. Revised enlarged – London, Clive Bingley, 1971, p.59-67, and 82. (ISBN 0-85157-118-2).

Two continuous sections included in Chapter 5: Alphabetical subject headings (p.54-83). For abstract, see #25. Added are a list of 20 types of operators and of ranking of subject fields in relation to locality name, both of which are reproduced from Coates' *Subject catalogues: headings and structure.* (KK)

#27 **Coates [and] Cross-reference structure** / A.C. Foskett – In his: *The subject approach to information,* 3rd ed. – London, Clive Bingley: Hamden, CT, Linnet Books, 1977, p.107-116, and 126. (ISBN 0-85157-238-3; 0-208-01546-9).

Two continuous sections included in Chapter 7: Alphabetical subject headings (p.102-126). For abstract, see #26. (KK)

#28 **Coates [and] Cross-reference structure** / A.C. Foskett – In his: *The subject approach to information,* 4th ed. – London, Clive Bingley: Hamden, CT, Linnet Books, 1982, p.128-138, and 148-149. (ISBN 0-85157-313-4; 0-208-01934-0).

Two continuous sections included in Chapter 7: Alphabetical subject headings: Cutter to Lynch (p.123-149). For abstract, see #26. Added is a description of the Current Technology Index (CTI) which replaced BTI in 1981. (KK)

#29 Coates [and] Cross-reference structure / A.C. Foskett – In his: *The subject approach to information,* 5th ed. – London, Library Association Publishing, 1996, p.130-132, and 145. (ISBN 1-85604-048-8).

Two continuous sections included in Chapter 8: Alphabetical subject headings: Cutter to Austin (p.123-146). For abstract, see #26. A description of Coates' theory of subject headings is reduced in size, e.g. a list of 20 types of operators is eliminated. Instead, added is a description of the Current Technology Index (CTI) which replaced BTI in 1981. (KK)

#30 E.J. Coates, the British Technology Index and the theory of subject headings: the man who loved cat springing / A.C. Foskett – In: *The variety of librarianship: essays in honour of John Wallace Metcalfe* / ed. W.B. Rayward – Sydney, Library Association of Australia, 1976, p.77-90. (ISBN 0-909915-42-3).

Based on a paper given at a PRECIS seminar, National Library of Australia, November 1974. Traces the historical development of subject indexing through the work of Cutter and Kaiser, leading to an assessment of the contribution of E.J. Coates, former editor of BTI. Once the idea is accepted that satisfactory indexing requires a complete statement of the subject of a document as a basis, the problem of how to formulate such a statement and how to treat it must be tackled. Cutter offered no firm answer and although Kaiser's 'concrete' and 'process' theory was a step forward, it has been overtaken by the increasing complexity of the literature that has to be indexed. How to cater for today's complex subjects still needs solving. Coates' idea of a systematic approach to subject headings is one way to answer. He started from the same point as Kaiser: the combination of a concrete and a process – a Thing and an Action, and the Thing takes precedence in the subject heading. Coates applies user psychology: people visualise things more easily than the actions performed on them, therefore users of the catalogue are more likely to look first under the concrete (thing) rather than the process. Discusses the application of these theories and the chain indexing procedure to the subject indexing of BTI and outlines the system of cross references. The effectiveness of BTI's indexing system is seen as the basis of its success as an international reference tool. (LISA 77/1845)

Prior to the paper there had been an unpublished typewritten document presented at the Seminar on PRECIS, National Library of Australia, 13-15 November 1974: *The man who loved cat springing* / A.C. Foskett – Canberra, National Library of Australia, 1974, 9p. (KK)

#31(#30) [Review of] The variety of librarianship: essays in honour of John Wallace Metcalfe / George M. Jenks – *Journal of Library History* (ISSN 0275-3650), 13(1)

Winter 1978, p.112-114.

Says that like most festschrifts the book suffers from the lack of a central theme. But 7 of the 11 essays are about subject classification, which is a most appropriate topic in this case. Of these the most readable is A.C. Foskett's essay on E.J. Coates, the *British Technology Index*, and the theory of subject headings. (KK)

#32 (#30)   [Review of] The variety of librarianship: essays in honour of John Wallace Metcalfe / S.D. Neill – *Library Quarterly* (ISSN 0024-2519), 48(1)January 1978, p.96-98.

There are seven papers on subject classification and four on libraries in Australia – both areas which have felt the strength of John Metcalfe. The reviewer has not accepted the order of table of contents but has devised a classification of chapters which is much more logical than the alphabetical-by-author melange adopted by the editor. Makes critical comment on every paper contributed, and recommends the book to all librarians, particularly to those interested in indexing and classification. As to a paper on Coates and BTI, the following comment is made: A.C. Foskett relates Cutter and Kaiser to the British Technology Index (BTI), axing Library of Congress Subject Headings along the way, in "E.J. Coates, the British Technology Index and the theory of subject headings." Foskett explains BTI chain procedure and pronounces it successful. (KK)

#33   Cutter to Austin / A.C. Foskett – *Cataloguing Australia* (ISSN 0312-4371), 2(3-4)July-December 1976, p.12-18.

Paper given at the Library Association of Australia Cataloguers' Section's national seminar '1876 and all that' held at Medlow Bath, September 1976. Reviews the development of alphabetical subject headings from Cutter to Austin. Cutter did for subject headings what Dewey did for classification. He propounded the idea of specific entry which however meant rather direct entry than now be understood. He recognized the importance of trying to select the right first word, and of using the natural form where possible. The Library of Congress gave tremendous influence on subject cataloguing practice, but a negligible influence on subject cataloguing theory. Cutter's principles had been developed in a rather different way on the other side of Atlantic. Kaiser argued that headings in an alphabetical catalogue were not natural language but an artificial one. He established the Concrete-Process order. Coates worked out a significant order, and discovered that it is in most cases the reverse order of the prepositional phrases denoting the subject. He drew up a list of 20 types of relationships and later had the opportunity to put his ideas into practice, i.e. he became the first editor of the *British Technology Index*. He also produced a system of cross-references which could be computerized. Austin solved the problem of incomplete cross-references found in chain procedure through PRECIS. The British Classification Research Group has suggested that all of the semantic relationships fall into one of the three groups: equivalence, hierarchy and affinitive/associative. Concludes that any developments that we see now were prompted by Cutter's work 100 years ago. (KK)

#34   **Facets, roles and cases** / W. John Hutchins – In: *Informatics 1: proceedings of a conference held by the Aslib Co-ordinate Indexing Group on 11-13 April 1973 at Durham University* / ed. K.P. Jones – London, Aslib, 1974, p.89-97. (ISBN 0-85142-058-3).

Describes that linguists have been interested in the deep 'case' relations of natural languages, e.g. 'agent,' 'patient,' 'beneficiary,' 'locative,' etc. and the way in which these relations are realized in the 'surface' forms of sentences. In classification and indexing, the identification of such syntagmatic relations is central to: facet analysis, the assignment of roles, problems of citation order, etc. The interests coincide in a number of respects and it is worthwhile to examine the differences and similarities of the various treatments proposed. Coates proposed that terms should be analyzed into categories such as 'Thing', 'Part', 'Material', 'Action' and 'Property' and cited in this order in subject headings. In the case of more complex headings, pairs of categories such as 'Action : Thing' are substituted for one category alone. The contribution of Coates is regarded as an attempt to establish helpful citation orders by semantic categorization of terms in conjunction with a syntactic analysis of prepositional phrases. It represents an attempt to relate the surface forms of natural language phrases to the underlying semantic relationships which they express. (KK)

#35   **Subject heading syntax and 'natural language' nominal compound syntax** / Thomas Lee Eichman – In: *The information age in perspective: proceedings of the ASIS Annual Meeting 1978, Volume 15 (41st Annual Meeting, New York, November 13-17, 1978)* / ed. Everett H. Brenner – White Plains, NY, Knowledge Industry Publications for the American Society for Information Science, 1978, p.126-129. (ISBN 0-9142-3622-9).

Briefly discusses the grammatical nature and functions of subject headings from a linguistic point of view, and reminds indexers that users can only treat headings as natural language. Lists 19 English natural language nominal compounds that almost exactly match the subject heading types created by E.J. Coates, and analyses how a user might employ his own experience of English to interpret an index containing these headings. Points out that the indexing system PRECIS, based on linguistic principles, produces syntactically natural entries, and urges close consideration of this system by indexers in the USA. (LISA 80/544)

#36   **Diary of visit to the U.K., November 30, 1963 – February 1, 1964** / John Wallace Metcalfe – In his: *Developing a profession of librarianship in Australia: travel diaries and other papers of John Wallace Metcalfe* / ed. W. Boyd Rayward – Lanham, MD, Scarecrow Press, 1995, p.224-296. (ISBN 0-8108-2944-4).

This is Chapter 9 of the book. While stayed in the U.K., Metcalfe visited the office of BTI to meet Coates on Friday, 13th December 1963. He regarded BTI as the result of compromise and economy, since there were both an attempt at a single-entry alphabetical index with cross-references and an attempt to maintain an appearance of classification and chain indexing method. In reading the introduction to the first annual volume of BTI, Metcalfe felt that there was a deliberate intention to be different not only in terminology but also in its method, which came down to Cutter's specific entry with ambiguities in punctuation and forms of cross-references. On Wednesday, 25th December 1963 Metcalfe started really to read Coates on "*Subject catalogues*." He says that the book should have been entitled, "A chain indexer's complete demolition of Cutter-Congress cataloguing," and regards it as the distortions of what Cutter wrote and thought. Points out that the book was just pre-BTI. (KK)

#37 **When is a subject not a subject?** / John Metcalfe – In: *Toward a theory of librarianship: papers in honor of Jesse Hauk Shera* / ed. Conrad H. Rawski – Metuchen, NJ, Scarecrow Press, 1973, p.303-338. (ISBN 0-8108-0535-9).

The subject of this essay is the meaning of 'subject' in systems of information retrieval (IR) and its understood or assumed meaning for those who use IR systems. Considers the concept of and the treatment of subject presented by Cutter, Kaiser, Ranganathan and Coates. Mention is particularly made of the principle of 'specific entry' which was originally advocated by Cutter. Complains that Coates makes nothing of Cutter's distinction of 'object' and 'aspect' and of Kaiser's 'concrete' and 'process' as a special use of this distinction, and that he goes straight from Kaiser to Ranganathan. Criticizes Ranganathan's chain procedure which was later adopted by Coates to the *British Technology Index*. Concludes that the word 'subject' is not a satisfactory term in IR systems because of its ambiguity, particularly with distinctions of general and specific, and of object and aspect. The author intends to go on distinguishing Cutter's 'object' and 'aspect'. (KK)

#38 **Information retrieval, British and American, 1876-1976** / John Metcalfe – Metuchen, NJ, Scarecrow Press, 1976, p.37, 88, 171-173, and 189-191. (ISBN 0-8108-0875-7).

Points out that according to Coates there are two possible conceptions of specific entry. The one favoured by Cutter envisages a set of stock subjects. The alternative one is Coates' subject heading made to measure, the subject co-extensive with the subject of the book. Argues that Coates' whole and only qualifying justification for alphabetico-specific entry may be still questioned. Reference is next made to chain procedure, which was used with indexing of classified cataloguing such as BNB and later purely alphabetical indexing as BTI. Stresses that though the latter case is much simpler than that of the former, chain procedure has the same defects. Cites an example from the 1962 Annual volume of BTI such as "COTTON, BLEACHING, HYDROGEN PEROXIDE." Points out that the user looking under Bleaching does not find a reference to "Breaching materials including Hydrogen peroxide" in the cross-references. (KK)

#39 Indexing the classified catalogue / Russell Sweeney – *Catalogue & Index* (ISSN 0008-7629), (19)July 1970, p.10-12.

Abridgement of a paper at the Spring Seminar, "Subject to Information," Aberystwyth, 1970. The alphabetical subject index, as part of the classified catalogue, needs re-examination. Ranganathan's chain procedure has had great influence. Questions arising from this technique's use are: (1) is the unassisted reader aware of the alphabetical subject index-classified file interaction; (2) are economic arguments powerful enough to warrant its use. Considers (1) from the viewpoints of a user's search for *fertilisers for wheat* and the little-known about users' subject formulations including Coates' Thing-Material-Action theory. For (2), the most satisfactory procedure would be full permutation. In special libraries this is out of the question but perhaps general librarians should not be over-persuaded by economics. A possibility would be to cycle the entry word and its immediate qualifier. Librarians' preferences may conflict with users' preferences and the assumption that generic-specific entries are not required in the alphabetical subject index should be questioned. (LISA 70/2038)

#40 A comparative study on the compound subjects by Foskett, Coates and Cutter [In Japanese] / Hisao Shimura – *Memoire of the Toshokan Tanki Daigaku* (ISSN 0385-4493), (8)1974, p.65-79.

C.A. Cutter's subject approach is considered in the light of his rules 161, 174 and 175. These rules were established for the treatment of subject headings in dictionary catalogue: (1) 161 for specific entry; (2) 174-175 for compound subjects; and (3) 174 for six patterns of subject heading form. Cutter's order of subject headings was almost that of natural language. E.J. Coates considered three most important elements in compound subjects: Thing-Material-Action, which was called 'Significance order.' He established 'Relationship table' and later applied to the British Technology Index. A.C. Foskett examined methods of the treatment of elements in compound subjects such as permutation, cycling and SLIC indexing, etc. (Original abstract amended by KK)

#41 Chain procedure and dictionary catalogue / T.V.R. Kumar and M. Parameswaran – *Library Science with a Slant to Documentation and Information Studies* (ISSN 0254-2553), 35(4)December 1998, p.241-246.

Explains the different types of subject entries in a dictionary catalogue. Examines the problems involved in the application of chain indexing procedure for deriving subject entries for dictionary catalogues. Discusses the modification of the rules of chain indexing procedure suggested by Coates, Ranganathan and Job. Concludes that since the human mind expects some kind of logical sequence, subject entries in a dictionary catalogue need to display some element of classified arrangement rather than a purely alphabetical sequence. (Original abstract)

10 PRENATAL STAGE AND EARLY YEARS OF BTI

10.10 Prospects for a new subject index to British technical journals

Annual report of the Council of the Association was an annual pamphlet published by the Library Association in London.
Liaison was a monthly newsletter inserted in the *Library Association Record.*

#42 **'IOTA' collapses** – *Liaison* (no ISSN), November 1958, p.196.

The *Index of Technical Articles* (IOTA) collapsed in September 1958. IOTA was another publishing venture that succeeded Cleaver-Hume's *Technical Article Index* that was published in 1952 modeled on the Norwegian *Artikkel Indeks.* Discusses the reason why IOTA has lost the support of subscribers. There were criticisms of IOTA. Prominent among these criticisms were the inadequacy of the subject arrangement and indexing, and the failure to publish in sections as Cleaver-Hume had done. IOTA earned praise as well as blame from librarians. But praise and regrets must be cold comfort to the publishers. (KK)

#43 **Index of Technical Articles** – *Aslib Proceedings* (ISSN 0001-253X), 11(1)January 1959, p.4.

Says that the Bureau of Technical Information Services Ltd. has suspended publication of the *Index of Technical Articles* (IOTA). The service of IOTA was announced in the December 1957 issue of this journal. IOTA was expected to be a useful service for special librarians and information workers, but did not find enough support to make it a sound business proposition. (KK)

#44 **I.O.T.A.** – *Library Association Record* (ISSN 0024-2195), 61(1)January 1959, p.1.

Describes the post mortems on the recent demise of the *Index of Technical Articles* (IOTA) which ran for a brief 20 issues. Points out that IOTA was the second venture of its kind to have failed in recent years. Enumerates several points emerged: (1) Continuity in the indexing of technical articles is of paramount importance; (2) The body organizing such an index should be one whose primary interest is not commercial, though such a venture should pay its way; (3) Any attempt to cover the whole fields of technology is too ambitious and unnecessary; and (4) An indexing service of this kind must decide that the appropriate Sections of LA should examine the possibility of a monthly index covering British scientific and technical articles and give realistic recommendations about it during 1959. (KK)

#45 **Publications. (iv) Index to technical periodicals** – *Annual report of the Council of the Association for the year ending 31st December, 1959: Presented at the annual meeting in Scarborough 1960* – London, Library Association, [1960], p.12.

Consideration was given to the possibility of producing a regular index to articles in about

350 British technical periodicals. It was clear that compilation and publication of the index would involve additional staff and a heavy financial commitment for the Association, and the matter was still under review at the end of 1959. (Original text)

#46   Publications. (v) Index to technical periodicals – *Annual report of the Council of the Association for the year ending 31st December, 1960: Presented at the annual meeting in Hastings 1961* – London, Library Association, [1961], p.10.

Further consideration was given to this project and a prospectus was prepared for issue early in 1961 to assess probable demand. (Original text)

#47   Talks with D.S.I.R. on technical periodicals index – *Liaison* (no ISSN), June 1960, p.46. See also #50.

Following the disappearance of Iota, a sub-committee of LA has been examining the financial and production matters concerning a similar new index of British technical periodicals. A list of 348 titles was compiled. It was assumed that 25,000 items would produce 50,000 entries per year and that the Varityper process would be employed for an edition of 1,000 copies of 11 monthly issues and an annual volume, the production cost of which would be about 18,000 pounds sterling. It was felt that the ultimate market should exceed 1,000 copies, but that over the first three years the index would run at a loss. The Secretary has been in touch with certain organizations, including DSIR, who might be interested in the proposed index to guarantee LA against possible loss. If a series of talks with DSIR confirm the need for such an index, DSIR would be willing to put down hard cash in seeing the index through its first three years. (KK)

#48   New periodicals / K.G.B. Bakewell – *Library Association Record* (ISSN 0024-2195), 63(3)March 1961, p.87. See also #56.

It is good to see that the Library Association proposes extending its activities in the field of periodical indexing and one hopes that *British technology index: a cumulative index to British technical periodicals* will be well supported. If sufficient support is forthcoming, the index will probably begin publication in January 1962 at £15 15s. per annum. It will be arranged alphabetically by subjects and will be published monthly, with a cumulated annual volume. (Original text)

#49   British Technology Index – *Nature* (ISSN 0028-0836), 189(4769)March 1961, p.969-970.

If sufficient support is forthcoming, a new endeavour is to be made to index the contents of about 400 British technical periodicals. There have been at least two earlier attempts to do this. Part of the reason for their failures was probably the absence of a cumulative volume. The new *Index* will have 11 monthly parts (no August issue) and a bound annual cumulation. It will be sponsored by the Library Association (LA). The time-lag of the *Index* will be within six weeks. The price will be about 15 guineas. Further particulars, and a prospectus containing a specimen page, are obtainable from LA in London. (KK)

#50 **British Technology Index in 1962: L.A. venture promised wide support –** *Liaison* (no ISSN), May 1961, p.33-34. See also #47.

Cautioned but not deterred by the earlier failure of the Cleaver-Hume's *Technical Article Index* and of *IOTA*, and undismayed by the scepticism of DSIR about its need, LA has determined to launch a *British Technology Index* in January 1962. The idea of BTI was put forward by John Frederick Walter Bryon in November 1958. In the finance and business management of publishing BTI, LA will have benefit of its experience in publishing the profitable *Subject Index to Periodicals*. Production of BTI will be done by the BNB Unit, using Varitypers. Chief deficiencies that BTI should overcome are problems of coverage and time-lag, and extremely broad classification and lack of cumulation from which Cleaver-Hume and IOTA had suffered. Several benefits of BTI are recognized. (KK)

#51 **British Technology Index** – *Library World* (ISSN 0024-2616), 62(731)May 1961, p.248.

LA has for some time been interested in publishing a successor to IOTA that was a commercially-run periodical but finally collapsed. LA's venture will be called the *British Technology Index* to be published in January 1962. The subscription will be 15 guineas per annum post free and BTI will be published by the BNB organization. BTI will be a landmark in the publishing history of LA. Appeals to British librarians for solid support as the potential support from libraries overseas is already encouraging. (KK)

#52 **British Technology Index** – *Unesco Bulletin for Libraries* (ISSN 0041-5243), 15(4) July-August 1961, p.216.

The Library Association, London, proposes, if sufficient support is received, to issue a monthly guide to the latest developments in British technology, under the title *British technology index*. The index will be in a single, alphabetical arrangement of subjects, with a cumulated annual volume, permitting the monthly parts to be discarded. It is intended initially to analyse about 400 British technological periodicals (over one-third of which are not currently abstracted elsewhere) and to produce 11 monthly issues, excluding August, and a bound annual cumulation. The subscription will be approximately £15.15s. ($50). It is hoped to begin publication in January 1962. Further information may be obtained from the Library Association, Chaucer House, Malet Place, London, W.C.1 (United Kingdom). (Original text)

#53 **New serials** – *Special Libraries* (ISSN 0038-6723), 52(8)October 1961, p.482.

British Technology Index: a cumulative index to British technical periodicals, is to be a monthly guide to latest developments in British technology. Listed alphabetically by subject, there will be a cumulated annual volume permitting monthly parts to be discarded. About 400 titles will be analysed. Publication is to begin in January 1962. The *Index* will be available from the Library Association, Chaucer House, Malet Place, London, W.C.1. for $50. (Original text)

#54   **Coates** – *Library Association Record* (ISSN 0024-2195), 63(8)August 1961, p.288.
   Mr. E.J. Coates, F.L.A., Chief Subject Cataloguer, *British National Bibliography*, to be Editor, *British Technology Index*. (Original text)

#55   **Coates is B.T.I. Editor** – *Liaison* (no ISSN), August 1961, p.61.
   The *British Technology Index* – the L.A.'s new publishing venture which commences in January 1962 – will be edited by Mr. E.J. Coates, at present chief subject cataloguer of the *British National Bibliography*. Mr. Coates will take up his duties at Chaucer House in September. (Original text)

#56   **[British Technology Index]** / K.G.B. Bakewell – *Library Association Record* (ISSN 0024-2195), 63(9)September 1961, p.312. See also #48.
   Would-be subscribers will now have received the prospectus for, and list of periodicals to be indexed in, the Library Association's *British technology index,* which I welcomed in my March notes and which will commence publication in January 1962. Most librarians will have some comments to make on the list of journals, and it is up to each of us to study his own field and inform Mr. Coates of any omissions. I feel that the layout could possibly be improved; the references might be more clearly set out, and *please, please, please,* will the Library Association set an example to others by using *standard* journal layout and *World list* abbreviations. (Original text)

#57   **Publications. (iv) British Technology Index** – *Annual report of the Council of the Association for the year ending 31st December, 1961: Presented at the annual meeting in Llandudno 1962* – London, Library Association, [1962], p.11.
   Early in 1961 a prospectus was circulated to librarians of all kinds outlining the scope of the proposed *British Technology Index* and asking for promises of subscriptions in the event of publication. This inquiry confirmed the Council's opinion that there was a real need for such a publication and that sufficient demand would be forthcoming, at home and abroad, to justify the Association undertaking this new venture. Arrangements were accordingly made for the publication of the first monthly issue of the Index to appear in February, 1962, and Mr. E.J. Coates was appointed as Editor. (Original text)

#58   **B.T.I. out in mid-February and new name for Subject Index** – *Liaison* (no ISSN), December 1961, p.97. See also #62.
   The first issue of the *British Technology Index* (BTI) is expected to be published in mid-

February 1962. This makes the title of the *Subject Index to Periodicals* that has been used since 1915 renamed the *British Humanities Index* from January 1962. In view of experience gained in producing BNB a dummy run to test all aspects of the monthly production process is not considered necessary. E.J. Coates, the first editor of BTI, reported to the Publication Committee that there had been a poorer response from industrial libraries in UK than had been hoped, and said that there might be an element of wait-and-see in this. Emphasizes that LA is not exclusively concerned with public libraries, and that BTI will not suffer the same fate nor make the same editorial mistakes the former Cleaver-Hume and IOTA have done. (KK)

#59 **The year ahead** / W.B. Paton – *Library World* (ISSN 0024-2616), 63(739) January 1962, p.156-157.

President of the Library Association (LA) says that several new ventures of LA will start in 1962. Most important of all is the inauguration of the *British Technology Index* (BTI). BTI is a major project in the LA's publishing programme, and one which they hope will gain wide national and international support. (KK)

#60 **British Technology Index** – *Nature* (ISSN 0028-0836), 193(4817) February 1962, p.727-728.

Introduces the upcoming *British Technology Index* (BTI) which should be regarded as a significant step towards rectifying the lack of adequate technical information service. Outlines the feature of BTI. Mentions that the functions of indexes and abstracts are to a certain extent complementary, and that BTI will be to bridge the time-lag between an article and its abstract when information may be untraceable. Expects that BTI and its American counterpart, i.e. the *Applied Science and Technology Index,* will give technologists and engineers reasonable facilities for keeping abreast of new developments. (KK)

#61 **British Technology Index** – *Library Resources & Technical Services* (ISSN 0024-2527), 6(1) Winter 1962, p.12.

Slated to begin publication this month is *British Technology Index, a Cumulative Index to British Technical Periodicals.* Published by The Library Association, Chaucer House, London, it is "intended initially to analyze about 400 titles, over one-third of which are not currently indexed or abstracted elsewhere." It is planned to appear in eleven monthly issues, excluding August, and a bound annual volume. The price is 15 guineas ($50). (Original text)

#61a **News from the field. Publications [British Technology Index]** – *College & Research Libraries* (ISSN 0010-0870), 23(2) March 1962, p.155.

British Technology Index, a cumulative index to British technical journals, began publication in January 1962. Initially 400 titles will be analyzed. The publication will appear monthly and will be cumulated annually. The publisher is the Library Association, Chaucer House, Malet Place, London, W.C. 1; price: 15 guineas ($50). (Excerpt from original text)

10.20 Scepticism and controversy

See also #50.

#62   British Technology Index / R.N. Beer – *Library Association Record* (ISSN 0024-2195), 64(2)February 1962, p. 65-66. See also #58.

Asks some questions concerning the statement of the editor of BTI that there had been a poorer response from industrial libraries in UK than had been hoped (*Liaison*, December 1961, p.97): (1) Did LA approach representatives of industrial libraries to find out their needs? (2) Is LA aware of the needs of technologists, technicians and applied scientists? (3) Does an index service measure up to the demands of applied scientists? Asks if there is great need for a publication entitled "British Technological Abstracts," which is compiled by a body of applied scientists, technicians, technologists and special librarians. Admits that such an undertaking requires support from various bodies such as industry, research associations, Aslib, IIS and DSIR, and asks LA what degree of cooperation would be forthcoming? (KK)

#63 (#62)   British Technology Index / L.L. Ardern – *Library Association Record* (ISSN 0024-2195), 64(2)February 1962, p. 66-67. See also #91.

As a member of the Sub-Committee, the author replies to questions raised by R.N. Beer and comments on them. Says that the Committee did seek advice from many potential users. Clears up the misunderstanding that BTI will take the place of abstracts since they serve another service. Agrees to the statement on the time-lag of subject indexes for abstracting services, and adds that the time-lag with BTI will be weeks. The Committee was influenced by the success of the *Applied Science and Technology Index* (ASTI), though it only covers about 200 periodicals, of which about 20 are British. The Committee did talk about an abstract service, but this could only be undertaken through a national information centre. Stresses that the members of the Council have faith in BTI and that time will show that BTI is filling a real need. (KK)

#64   Human Rats [Reading, analysing, translating, selecting] / D.J. Urquhart – *Journal of Documentation* (ISSN 0022-0418), 19(3)September 1963, p.95-99.

A research worker keeps abreast of scientific information in three ways: (1) he may spend many hours a week in reading for keeping up to date or looking for specific information; (2) his reading is selected by a technical information officer in his firm library; (3) he does little reading because of no library there. Unless a publication is mentioned in a guide to literature, it is not likely to be asked for. Machines cannot make a major contribution until one is produced which can be read automatically, analyse and translate mechanically, and select mechanically; such a machine (RATS) is not likely to appear in the near future. Until such a machine is realized, manual techniques must be improved. Libraries should concentrate not on helping users but on helping them to help themselves. As to BTI that is LA's new venture, says that commercial success is not a test for its usefulness. Emphasizes that the question of whether BTI is really useful is a complex one and that it includes many questions. Cautions that we must not be under the delusion that BTI is a cheap publication for its contents. Compares the price of BTI with that of *Chemical Abstracts*. (KK)

#65(#64) **'Human Rats'** / L.L. Ardern – *Journal of Documentation* (ISSN 0022-0418), 20(1) March 1964, p.53.

This is a critical comment on Urquhart's statements on BTI. Makes an objection to wrong interpretation on the usefulness of BTI. Points out some mistakes concerning the matters on BTI. (KK)

#66(#105) **Monitoring current technical information** / H.P. Cemach – *Aslib Proceedings* (ISSN 0001-253X), 15(3) March 1963, p.91-92. See also #105.

Editor of the ANBAR Documentation Service on Office Organization, Management and Methods makes a few comments on Coates' paper (*Aslib Proceedings*, 14(12) December 1962, p.426-437). While they have experienced similar range of problems and have in many cases come to similar conclusions, they have some different conclusions as to: (1) journal coverage, (2) criteria for articles included, and (3) speed of publication. Concludes that Coates has given them food for a lot of thought, and that what would be so welcome and so valuable is users' view on these points. (KK)

#67(#66) **Monitoring current technical information** / E.J. Coates – *Aslib Proceedings* (ISSN 0001-253X), 15(4) April 1963, p.131.

Editor of BTI agrees with Cemach that a discussion on the points he raised would be useful. Suggests that it is not altogether helpful to attempt to comparative evaluation of services and index structures which serve differing purposes. The purposes determine the priorities in each case. Gives an account of the different functions between abstract and index. There are considerations which lead the BTI to attach importance first to currency of entries, and secondly to objective and easily understood criteria in determining selection of material for inclusion. As to the danger of falling between two stools, i.e. single sequence alphabetical and subject grouped plus alphabetical index, points out that one needs only note the virtual disappearance of the alphabetico-classed form of index. (KK)

#68(#67) **Monitoring current technical information** / A.H. Holloway – *Aslib Proceedings* (ISSN 0001-253X), 15(6) June 1963, p.195.

Doubts Coates' letter that abstracts are intended for perusal and subject index occupies a comparatively low place in their scheme of priorities. Argues that abstracts are intended both for current awareness and for retrospective searching. Says that BTI is essentially a tool for current awareness, and that a different approach is needed for retrospective searching such as the index volume of *Chemical Abstracts*. (KK)

#69(#68) **Monitoring current technical information** / E.J. Coates – *Aslib Proceedings* (ISSN 0001-253X), 15(8)August 1963, p.243.

In reply to Holloway's criticism, says that most abstracting services do not issue concurrent subject indexes with abstracts and that it seems reasonable to describe the situation as one in which comparatively low priority is given to subject indexing. On the question of retrospective searching, notes that Holloway has felt able to make an evaluative comparison of the indexes to *Chemical Abstracts* with BTI, even though the first BTI volume for retrospective search had not yet appeared at the time when he wrote. (KK)

#70 **The British Technology Index: a preliminary evaluation** / R. Hindson – *Library Association Record* (ISSN 0024-2195), 65(6)June 1963, p.227-228.

Summarizes a few previous reviews of BTI. Enumerates some points, which the reviewer regards as drawbacks of BTI, such as (1) the coverage of British literature compared with specialized information services; (2) usage of terms in subject headings; (3) lack of standard bibliographical description, particularly abbreviation of periodical titles; and (4) problem of bibliographical scatter. Despite these drawbacks the reviewer regards BTI as being useful for borderline material, i.e. a most desirable tool for a small organization, and a general reference tool in technological information work. To conclude, suggests that some matters for improvement in BTI, such as the coverage, the subject indexing, the time-lag, and the summer gap. (KK)

#71(#70) **The Editor comments** / E.J. Coates – *Library Association Record* (ISSN 0024-2195), 65(6)June 1963, p.228-229.

In reply to Hindson, Editor of BTI stresses that the suggestion for more coverage and more frequent publication does require further cost. Makes a critical comment on the problem of: (1) coverage compared with that of abstracting service; (2) incidence of errors; (3) abbreviation of journal titles; (4) bibliographical scatter; and (5) summer gap that is now eliminated. (KK)

#72(#70) **British Technology Index** / P.R. Lewis – *Library Association Record* (ISSN 0024-2195), 65(8)August 1963, p.309-310. See also #181.

Citing Hindson's remark that "there is a peculiar alphabetico-classed effect in places," the author argues that BTI has been designed not as an alphabetical index but as a classification of technical articles. After the death of the *Index of Technical Articles* (IOTA) it was generally agreed that any new indexing service for technical articles should not be classified but alphabetical. Asserts that the only differences between BTI and IOTA are that the former's classification techniques are more sophisticated. In illustration of the assertion, uses an imaginary metamorphosis of the *British National Bibliography* (BNB) where the class numbers are abandoned. Points out that the first term in each heading of BTI is always that which stands for the "main class" never that which stands for specific subject, and that the logic of BTI is the logic of the classificationist and not of the indexer. (KK)

#73(#72) **British Technology Index** / E.J. Coates – *Library Association Record* (ISSN 0024-2195), 65(8)August 1963, p.310. See also #181.

Confirms Lewis' argument as follows: BTI headings have a classificatory basis of some sort, therefore BTI is a classified index. Agrees to the premise but considers the conclusion is false. Explains how BTI headings are related to faceted classification that gives predictive rules. With the appearance of the first Annual volume of BTI, concludes that the editor doubts if any comparable service has been more informative and explicit about its working methods in so short a time. (KK)

#74(#73) **British Technology Index** / P.R. Lewis – *Library Association Record* (ISSN 0024-2195), 65(11)November 1963, p.432.

Argues that every student nowadays knows the difference between alphabetical and classified forms, and that each depends for their working principles upon both an alphabetical list of terms and a classification of the subjects which the terms represent. Thinks that it is largely a matter of personal prejudice, rather than absolute efficiency, which decides the final form. Emphasizes that what makes BTI unique in its day is its unacknowledged attempt to be simultaneously alphabetical and classified, and that this sort of dual arrangement used to be called an "alphabetico-classed" index, as Hindson has reminded the reader. (KK)

#75(#72, #74) **British Technology Index** / E.J. Coates – *Library Association Record* (ISSN 0024-2195), 65(11)November 1963, p.433.

Says that there is an indirect relation between the BTI alphabetical structure and faceted classification structure. But denies Lewis' two descriptions of BTI: "classification of technical articles" (first letter) and "alphabetico-classed index" (second letter), which tallies with reality. To illustrate this discussion, suggests Lewis to recast the three index examples cited in his letter to give what he regards as a appropriate direct (and equally specific) form. Stresses that an index should not attempt to be simultaneously alphabetical and classified, and that it will be apparent to most people that no such attempt is made in BTI. (KK)

#76(#74) **British Technology Index** / W. Ashworth – *Library Association Record* (ISSN 0024-2195), 65(11)November 1963, p.433.

Mentions that it is difficult when setting up a small specialized library to select the best means for organizing the retrieval of information, and that a certain amount of internal indexing will prove inevitable. Suggests that the first Annual volume of BTI offers a new and neat solution to the problem of a small technical information unit. Argues that the form of subject headings, which P.R. Lewis claims that they owe something to classificatory principles, is not really material. The important point is, as Coates points out in his reply, that concrete predictable rules have been drawn up to achieve consistency. But these rules are much complex than indicated in the introduction to the Annual volume. Recommends to read Coates' *"Subject catalogues: headings and structure"* (1960), where the principles are fully explained. (KK)

#77(#76) **British Technology Index** / P.R. Lewis – *Library Association Record* (ISSN 0024-2195), 66(1)January 1964, p.37-38.

Comments on Ashworth's saying that what matters as to BTI's heading is its achievement of consistency by concrete predictive rules. Says that consistency is not the only one, and that intelligibility is another. Argues that the consistency achieved by the BTI indexers is paid for by the user in terms of clarity and ease of reference, which is a grave fault in indexing. Quotes one of BTI subject headings, and regards it to be not intelligible to the typical user even if reading Coates' *"Subject catalogues: headings and structure"* that Ashworth considers an essential prerequisite to the attempt. Maintains that the system Coates has invented for BTI was a classified index masquerading as an alphabetical one, and that it would be better if BTI turned itself properly into one or the other. (KK)

#78(#77) **British Technology Index** / E.J. Coates – *Library Association Record* (ISSN 0024-2195), 66(1)January 1964, p.38.

Mr. Lewis has been asked twice to tell us what he means by the "true" or "proper" indexing he would like *B.T.I.* to adopt. This is particularly necessary in connection with the three offending headings he selected in his second letter. His silence on this point is more significant than the continuing barrage of the last paragraph. I confirm (1) that *B.T.I.* is not a classified index, (2) that I do not follow Mr. Lewis through the hairpin bends of an argument which lead him to the contrary conclusion. Mr. Ashworth recommended *Subject Catalogues* to indexers wishing to follow *B.T.I.* practice. Mr. Lewis makes the recommendation apply to searchers in *B.T.I.* This is a fair example of his technique in attacking *B.T.I.* (Original text)

#79(#77) **British Technology Index** / J.R. Sharp – *Library Association Record* (ISSN 0024-2195), 66(2)February 1964, p.73-76.

Comments on the letters from P.R. Lewis on BTI. Says that readers are still waiting for a constructive suggestion as to what an alphabetical index should be look like. Points out that Lewis attempted to give the nature of BTI headings can be seen to be the same as the chains of terms comprising the subject headings of BNB, but the false contention can be supported by neither fact nor theory. Argues that Lewis does not understand the alphabetico-classed index. Discusses the feature which determines the nature of an alphabetico-classed index in some detail. Criticizes Lewis for his unfair attitude. Concludes that Coates had made to the philosophy of alphabetical cataloguing, and that it is a grave injustice that the consequences of his work have been little else but denigration. Finally, the editor of the *Library Association Record* declares the closure of a series of this correspondence. (KK)

#80(#77, #79) **1964: What were they saying then?** – *New Library World* (ISSN 0307-4803), 85(1006)April 1984, p.64-65.

This is the first of a series of excerpts from professional journals of two decades back. Points out that technical matters, particularly classification, cataloguing and indexing, were discussed in straight language and with a certain disrespect for persons. Quotes P.R. Lewis' remark on BTI in the Jan 64 *Record*, "The essence of my case against the *British technology index* is that the consistency achieved by the indexers is paid for entirely by the user in terms of clarity and ease of reference, and this I hold to be a grave fault in indexing." He was then chief cataloguer and bibliographer, Board of Trade Library. J.R. Sharp, then Deputy Librarian & Information Officer, British Nylon Spinners retorted in the Feb 64 *Record*, "Mr Lewis has been quick to attribute lack of understanding to Mr Coates (then editor of BTI), but it is clear from his arguments that he does not himself understand the nature of the one thing he has talked about so much – the alphabetico-classed index." (KK)

#81 **The L.A. Conference at Birmingham: 'Intimate, friendly, relaxed and unfettered'** / Jack Dove – *Library World* (ISSN 0024-2616), 66(771)September 1964, p.54-58 (esp. p.58).

The following is included in the author's report of the annual meeting of the Library Association (LA) held in Birmingham, 1964. Mr. [W.S.] Haugh told the author that the new LA building would be completed by May 1965 and Mr. [Kenneth Aldridge] Mallaber gave details of much improved library accommodation therein although it was not big enough in his view. Mentions that Mr. Mallaber also strongly resisted the idea of any further LA sponsored periodicals indexes. He reminds them that there is a *Public Affairs Index Service* originated in America and that the *British Technology Index* cost £20,000. (KK)

10.30 Reviews of monthly issue

#82 **British Technology Index: a current subject-guide to articles in British technical journals. Vol.1, No.1** / ed. E.J. Coates – London, Library Association, January 1962-, 70p. Annual subscription, £15.15s (Distributed in USA by R.R. Bowker, $50).

Below are 12 reviews, one of which is written in French. (KK)

#83(#82)   Technology index [Review] / Ferdinand Fathom – *British Books* (no ISSN), 176(4881)April 1962, p.20.

Mentions that the most important publishing venture ever undertaken by the Library Association is the *British Technology Index* (BTI) and that the potential usefulness of BTI can be no doubt. Describes the coverage and up-to-dateness of BTI. Admitting that the reviewer to be impatient, expresses a feeling of irritation and frustration to the 'see' and 'see also' references. Argues that over-signposting of cross-references can be expensive as well as irritating, and suggests that headings for related terms should be printed once a year only in a separate list. Adds that BTI has already proved its value to the reviewer apart from these minor faults mentioned above. (KK)

#84(#82)   [Review of monthly issue] / K.J. Spencer – *Library Association Record* (ISSN 0024-2195), 64(4)April 1962, p.153.

Since the IOTA ceased in August 1958, there has not been the means to obtain a comprehensive coverage of British technical journals. Following an outline of the first issue of BTI, some drawbacks of the present form are pointed out: (1) there are prolific "see" references and incomplete related headings that should be complemented in the annual cumulation; (2) an author index should be included in the annual cumulation; (3) bibliographic detail lacks the last page of an article and the number of references cited; and (4) titles in the periodicals list are not in every case as given in the references and appear not to comply with standard practice. Despite these drawbacks, the reviewer is confident of the overall efficiency and usefulness of BTI. (KK)

#85(#82)   [Review of monthly issue] [In French] / Anne-Marie Boussion – *Bulletin des Bibliotheques de France* (ISSN 0006-2006), 7(5)Mai 1962, p.319-320.

The *British Technology Index* is an alphabetical subject index to articles from about 400 technological periodicals published in UK. A list of selected journals, which must probably be all the technical periodicals in UK, is given in the first issue. As the coverage is limited to British journals, the index has eliminated many of the difficulties encountered by bibliographers in the exploration and acquisition of foreign journals. The index has also eliminated the risk of incomprehension or mistranslation in the analysis of documents. The index has two advantages: promptness and exhaustiveness. It is obvious that this form of bibliography, while not competed with large international bibliographies, provides current information, and that it would be of help to encourage other countries to undertake such a bibliography. (KK)

#86(#82)   British Technology Index [Review] / J. Farradane – *Journal of the Royal Institute of Chemistry* (ISSN 0368-3958), 86(5)May 1962, p.213-214.

Describes that BTI deals with a field that, in respect of engineering at least, has long had inadequate coverage. It is an alphabetical index to papers from some 400 British journals in engineering and chemical technology, and they are listed by subject keywords together with sub-keywords. For quick guidance to up-to-date literature, technologists may find this index very useful. Points out that the chief difficulty with this type of index is to a considerable extent overcome by extensive cross-referencing and duplicate entry almost to the point of excess, and that several matters should be improved. Concludes that further experience in production of this journal will remove blemishes. (KK)

#87(#82) **British Technology Index [Review]** / L. Dawn Pohlman – *Library Journal* (ISSN 0000-0027), 87(10)May 1962, p.1880.

Following a description of the coverage of BTI, the reviewer says that it will be a valuable supplement to technical indexes already in use. Points out that all the substantive articles relating to technical processes have been adequately indexed, while cover to cover indexing is not the intention of the publisher. Specific subject headings are composed of significant terms. In most cases there is a cross reference to the main subject from each of these components. Argues that this is a relatively inexpensive index, comprehensive, easy to use, and physically well-planned. (KK)

#88(#82) **New periodicals of 1962 – Part I [Review of monthly issue]** / James R. Thrash – *College & Research Libraries* (ISSN 0010-0870), 23(5)September 1962, p.410 and 418.

British Technology Index, published by the Library Association, provides a current subject guide to articles in the British technical journals and is, in short, the British equivalent to *[Applied] Science and Technology Index*. (Excerpt from original text)

#89(#82) **[Review of monthly issue]** / W.T. Singleton – *Ergonomics* (ISSN 0014-0139), 5(4)October 1962, p.587.

This new publication is intended to cover British journals dealing with all aspects of engineering and technology including ergonomics, work study, economics and management. An alphabetical subject list is used to classify articles for which title and author only are given. (Original text)

#90(#82) **[Review of monthly issue]** / Robert E. Burton – *Library Resources & Technical Services* (ISSN 0024-2527), 7(1)Winter 1963, p.124-125.

Raises some questions about BTI, including lack of an author index. Estimates the usefulness of BTI coverage by checking against those of the *Applied Science and Technology Index* and the *Engineering Index*. While acknowledges the specific and elaborate subject headings, finds faults with cross-references produced by chain procedural method. Two major problems concerning wording and spelling in subject headings are pointed out from the viewpoint of the use of BTI in USA. Concludes that BTI will be of utility in the library needing full access to British technical journals and that its usefulness will be increased if an author index is prepared and the inconsistencies in indexing and cross-referencing are eliminated. (KK)

#91 (#82)   **British Technology Index [Review]** – *Nature* (ISSN 0028-0836), 194 (4823) April 1962, p.15. See also #63.

In *British Technology Index* the Library Association has issued a valuable current subject guide to articles in British technical journals. 402 periodicals were covered in the first issue. Delays through the postal dispute excluded a further 120 periodicals to be covered in this issue. Entries are arranged alphabetically by subject, with adequate and common-sense cross-references, and are limited to title and bibliographical details. Among the features that should commend the *Index* to the industrial and technological user is the marked reduction in time-lag. In this connexion it is worth directing attention to the effective reply of L.L. Ardern in the *Library Association Record* for February to some questions asked about the response to the *Index* from industrial libraries in UK. (KK)

#92 (#82)   **[Review of monthly issue]** – *Journal of the Institution of Electrical Engineers* (ISSN 0368-2692), 8 (89) May 1962, p.266.

The aim of this monthly subject guide to articles in British technical journals is to provide the technologist with an index to what is currently being published in his field. (Original text)

#93 (#82)   **[Review of monthly issue]** – *Royal Society of Health Journal* (ISSN 0035-9130), 82 (3) May 1962, p.147.

Published for the first time in January 1962, this is a monthly guide to developments in British technology. The index is arranged alphabetically in subjects, giving the title of the relevant article, the author and the date of the periodical concerned. Eleven monthly issues (August excluded) will appear each year, and a bound annual volume. (Original text)

#94 (#82)   **[Review of monthly issue]** – *Unesco Bulletin for Libraries* (ISSN 0041-5243), 16 (6) November-December 1962, p.309.

This monthly index lists articles in British technical periodicals, arranged alphabetically under specific subject headings. The main subjects covered are: engineering, chemical technology, mining, metallurgy, metal manufactures, wood manufactures, textiles, clothing, papermaking, packaging works management, industrial economics of particular industries, industrial health and safety, technical education. Bibliographical details include article title, author, title of periodical, volume, date, pages, illustrations and references. A list of 351 British technical periodicals indexed is included. (Original text)

10.40 Reviews of annual volumes

#95   British Technology Index. Annual volume 1962 / ed. E.J. Coates – London, Library Association, 1963-, 902p. Full service, 12 monthly issues and annual volume £15.15s; Separate annual volume £9.9s (Distributed in USA by R.R. Bowker, $50 and $30 respectively).

   Annual volume of BTI was published in July the next year. Below are 8 reviews, one of which is written in Spanish. (KK)

#96(#95)   B.T.I. volume [Review] – *Liaison* (no ISSN), August 1963, p.56.

   Introduces the first annual volume of the *British Technology Index* (BTI) published in July 1963. It includes 28,000 subject entries, with about 50,000 cross-references. Emphasizes that BTI enables users to locate specific information with a minimum of time and efforts, and that a brief introduction to the indexing principles and syntax employed appears to break new ground in the developing literature on this subject. BTI is one of the LA's biggest publishing ventures, and it was agreed to subsidize BTI for a three-year period, half of which has now passed. Subscriptions for 1963 have now reached a total of 1,051, but to cover costs by next June will necessitate an increase in income of about £2,700. (KK)

#97(#95)   British Technology Index [Review] – *Aslib Proceedings* (ISSN 0001-253X), 15(10)October 1963, p.279.

   The first annual cumulation of BTI is now available. Following the format of its monthly parts, it lists about 28,000 entries for technical articles in 400 British journals. The subject coverage embraces all departments of engineering and chemical technology, together with the various manufacturing processes based upon them. It also includes a great deal of material on the pure science of man-made objects and industrial processes, although the main emphasis is on applied science. This 1962 cumulation will have been received by subscribers to the full service of the BTI, but may be obtained as a separate volume from the Library Association, price 9 guineas. (KK)

#98(#95)   [Review of annual volume] / K.C. Harrison – *Library World* (ISSN 0024-2616), 65(762)December 1963, p.220.

   The first annual volume of BTI is a landmark in the history of periodical indexing. It offers an opportunity to congratulate the editor (Mr. E.J. Coates) and his staff on a major achievement. They have made to ensure the accuracy and prompt appearance of BTI since its inception. The volume contains a brief introduction for users, annual cumulation and a list of journals indexed. BTI is still hardly a paying proposition and it behooves all librarians to give it the maximum support. Those who have been wavered will be convinced of the importance of this index if they will examine this first annual volume. BTI is going to have a scarcity value in the future. (KK)

#99(#95) **[Review of annual volume]** / Barbara Johnston – *Australian Library Journal* (ISSN 0004-9670), 12(4) December 1963, p.200.

Argues that to access an index to periodicals the number, quality and availability of the journals covered, the convenience of the arrangement and the speed of publication have to be considered. A comparison of BTI with the *Applied Science and Technology Index* (ASTI) shows the latter to cover 215 journals of which only 19 are British, so the production of BTI is justified. Mention is made of characteristics of subject headings. Points out that the physical form is first class. Concludes that LA has earned the gratitude of all those who use technical journals. (KK)

#100(#95) **British Technology Index [Review]** – *Special Libraries* (ISSN 0038-6723), 54(8) October 1963, p.536.

The Library Association, London, has published its first annual volume of *British Technology Index*, a 900-page volume covering all major articles in 400 British 1962 technical journals in the fields of engineering, chemical, and manufacturing technology. The volume, which is part of a service including monthly subject indexes, includes 28,000 subject entries having about 50,000 cross references. (Original text)

#101(#95) **[Review of annual volume]** – *Special Libraries* (ISSN 0038-6723), 54(10) December 1963, p.662.

First annual cumulative volume of the *British Technology Index*, which has appeared monthly since the beginning of 1962. 28,000 entries relating to technical articles, cross-indexed by subject, from 400 British journals in all areas of engineering and chemical technology. Index of journals. The subscription rate for full service (12 monthly parts and annual volume) is $50. (Original text)

#102(#95) **[Review of annual volume]** / C.G. Wood – *Library Review* (ISSN 0024-2535), 19(149) Spring 1964, p.353-354.

Argues that the requisite reading to accompany this annual volume is the editor's exposition of the objectives of BTI that was presented at the Aslib Conference, Blackpool, 1962, giving in detail subject heading syntax, retrieving power potential and extent of coverage offered by BTI. Based on random checking a few minor blemishes concerning related heading are pointed out. Recognizes that 'See' references using chain indexing procedure results in agglomerations. Regards BTI as to be suited to some users better than others. There is criticism from one quarter that disavows the usefulness of the project in its form. Such evaluations will go on until the accumulation of annual volumes on the shelves, but the important factor for many practitioners in information services is that BTI is now here. (KK)

#103 **[Review of annual volume]** [In Spanish] / T. Arends – *Acta Científica Venezolana*

(ISSN 0001-5504), 16(2)1965, p.84. The following is reviewed:

British Technology Index. Annual volume 1963 / ed. E.J. Coates – London, Library Association, 1964, 995p.

This book constitutes a subject index to most important articles in 400 British technical journals published in 1963. It is a large volume that comprises about 30,000 bibliographic entries arranged alphabetically by subject, together with cross-references. This book undoubtedly represents a tremendous achievement and is accomplished by the editor and four specialists. Like those responsible for the edition, the Library Association of Great Britain is to be congratulated. The lithographic product is excellent. It is a very useful reference book for those interested in the technological subjects of literature in English. (Akira Ueda)

20 ASPECTS OF BTI

20.10 General description

#104 **British Technology Index** / E.J. Coates – *Library Journal* (ISSN 0000-0027), 87(13) July 1962, p.2482-2484 (includes a portrait of the author).

This is the first paper on BTI written by the editor. (KK)

The editor of BTI sketches the background to the publication of this index, and indicates its scope and the type of articles indexed. The alphabetical subject arrangement is based on the assumption that there is greater need for an index capable of providing a swift answer to specific inquiries than for a compilation primarily suited to broad field browsing and survey. The principles underlying the structure of compound headings used in the index are explained and illustrated by examples. The index is printed by the same non-conventional techniques used for producing *BNB*. (LSA 62/12526)

#105 **Monitoring current technical information with the British Technology Index** / E.J. Coates – *Aslib Proceedings* (ISSN 0001-253X), 14(12)December 1962, p.426-437 (includes discussion, p.437). For comments on the paper, see #66 to #69.

The aim of BTI which covers 400 British technological journals, is to print entries as soon as possible for monthly publication, and to make the index as efficient as possible for retrieval. The journals were selected from those suggested by libraries circularized, and are reviewed every six months. Engineering and chemical technology and their manufacturing techniques comprise the main field; medicine and agriculture are excluded. The articles are still three or four times too many but by adopting rules for the exclusion of such material as one page articles they are reduced to what is possible. Nine-tenths of the entries appear within seven weeks of their original appearance. This will soon be true of all entries. This is probably the index's chief justification; nothing else equals it. Outline the fundamentals of

BTI's indexing directed to specificity. Entry is under application rather than process. The alphabetical form is useful for specific entries; it is laborious for broad field study. Even if a library's index is equally good it is useful for keeping up with fringe subjects. (LSA 63/13033)

Paper presented at the 36th Aslib Annual Conference held in Blackpool, October 1962. The author shows the index desiderata of the three attributes which determine the utility of a bibliographical index: (1) coverage; (2) currency; and (3) retrieving power. The word "monitoring" used in this paper indicated a middle activity between specific searching and primary stimulation, i.e. the regular brief systematic surveillance of what is currently going on in a narrow subject sector of particular interest. (KK)

#106 **Aims and methods of the British Technology Index** / E.J. Coates – *Indexer* (ISSN 0019-4131), 3(4) Autumn 1963, p.146-152. Reprinted in: *Indexers on indexing: a selection of articles published in The Indexer* / ed. Leonard Montague Harrod for the Society of Indexers – New York, Bowker, 1978, p.240-246. (ISBN 0-8352-1099-5). See also #151,

Up-to-date knowledge in a special field nowadays calls simultaneous awareness of what is going on in several other fields. There is therefore great need for indexes and other information processing compilations. BTI is concerned with applied science except medicine and agriculture, and covers 400 British technical journals each month with a subject index to 2-3,000 articles, most having appeared within the preceding seven weeks. BTI is intended to fill the gap of three months immediately following publication when there is no record of them at all, and the longer period before annual subject indexes to abstracts appear. Alphabetical specific subject arrangement is used. Two types of cross referencing multi-word index entries are explained; the inversion reference; and those directing the enquirer from a general to a more restricted heading. The citation order of the elements in composite headings should be predictable to users. They are generally arranged in order of decreasing concreteness, 15 distinct varieties of composite heading (of which 10 are proving to be important) have been isolated. In the first five, one term is a Thing, and the other specifies a particular kind or variety of the Thing. The other five important types of heading are concerned with properties and actions upon things and by things. Synonyms are generously referenced and new concepts referred to their context in library classification schemes. Homonyms cause problems, the solution to which is so far inconsistent with mechanical alphabetical order. There is a staff of four library qualified indexers and two clerical workers. The indexing organization is described. So far it has not been possible to devise a series of simple instructions needed to put the clerical work on to a computer. (LSA 63/13798)

#107 (#106) **The Indexer: thirty years ago** – *Indexer* (ISSN 0019-4131), 18(4) October 1993, p.243.

Volume 3, Number 4 of *The Indexer*, the autumn 1963 issue, was the last edited by John Thornton. He welcomed his successor, L.M. Harrod. Three highly distinguished indexers came to the fore in this issue. A.R. Hewitt wrote nine expert pages on legal indexing, on which he subsequently published classic volumes. E.J. Coates described 'Aims and methods of the *British Technology Index*'. M.D. Anderson made two contributions, writing of 'Indexers at play' and 'The indexer as proof corrector.' (KK)

#108 **Introduction** / E.J. Coates – In: *British Technology Index. Annual volume 1962* – London, Library Association, 1963, p.v-ix. See also #268.

Introduction to BTI Annual volume 1962 gives an account of: subject scope; index structure; order of elements in headings (as its basics are presented in the BTI Relationship Table); indexing of locality terms; journals covered; selection of articles; and so on. Introduction to annual volume 1963, 1968, 1969, 1972 and 1979 should also be looked through. (KK)

#109 **Bibliographical organization and bibliographies** / A.J. Walford – In: *Five years' work in librarianship, 1961-1965* / ed. P.H. Sewell – London, Library Association, 1968, p.471-506 (esp. p.496).

British technology index (1962-, monthly), which began publication as a calculated financial risk, has established itself as an indispensable tool for British libraries. The promptness of its monthly appearance vies with that of the U.S. *Applied science and technology index*, but its "chain" subject headings have provoked some criticism. (Excerpt from original text)

#110 **B.T.I. is biggest** – *Liaison* (no ISSN), November 1965, p.74.

This is a general description of BTI as of late in 1965. Topics touched upon are: the location of BTI editorial office (Argyle House, Euston Road); the reason of a new indexing service; a streamlined indexing technique and necessary indexing skill for the work; the number of entries in both monthly issue and annual volume; the number of subscribers and the 'breakeven' point for BTI; OSTI's grant for a feasibility study on computerization of the clerical works; and a plan for computer typesetting of printout in detail. (KK)

#111 **[Outline of BTI as of 1966]** – *Indexer* (ISSN 0019-4131), 5(2)Autumn 1966, p.103.

British Technology Index, which was started in 1962, is the biggest of the Library Association's single publishing ventures. It indexes periodicals in the pure and applied science fields which are not adequately covered in existing indexes, and in the preparation of the 30,000 entries per annum, four hundred British technical journals are scanned. Each month about 2,200 entries are recorded, and so great is the development in scientific knowledge that about 1,500 new subject headings have to be prepared monthly. (Original text)

#112 **British Technology Index** / E.J. Coates – In: *Encyclopedia of library and information science*, Vol.3 / ed. A. Kent et al. – New York, Marcel Dekker, 1970, p.327-341.

This is the most comprehensive description of BTI by its editor. Topics covered are: bibliographic outline; background of the commencement of technical indexing service; preliminary research; construction of subject headings; inversion cross-references; vocabulary control; computerization and typesetting; possibility of extended services brought about by computerization; and the significance of BTI. There is a wealth of the literature on BTI written by Coates. (KK)

#113 **British Technology Index** [In Japanese] / Keiichi Kawamura – In his: *Subject indication for information retrieval: the contributions of Eric Coates* – Tokyo, Nichigai Associates, 1988, p.55-143. (ISBN 4-8169-0774-2).

This book is the most comprehensive study on the work of Eric Coates ranging from 1960 to 1987. It consists of three parts: (1) Development of the theory of subject headings; (2) British Technology Index (BTI); and (3) Broad System of Ordering (BSO). The second part (2) consists of the following seven chapters: Background and development; Subject heading syntax; Vocabulary control; Computerization project; Indexing methodology after computerization; Index pages; and The value of BTI. (KK)

20.20 Coverage

#114 **Index values** / Bernard Houghton and Glyn Rowland – *New Library World* (ISSN 0307-4803), 73(866)August 1972, p.363-364.

Presents data on overlap/underlap in the coverage of *ASTI, BTI* and *EI* gathered by students at Liverpool Polytechnic School of Librarianship. The services combined cover 2,390 titles; *EI* covers 2,205; *BTI* 342; and *ASTI* 227. The number of titles covered in 1 service and not in the other 2 is: *EI* 1,845; *BTI* 175; *ASTI* 11. Overlap between *BTI* and *EI* is 167 titles; that between *ASTI* and *EI* is 214 titles; and that between *BTI* and *ASTI* is 3. Observations are made on time lag (*BTI* 3-7 weeks, *ASTI* and *EI* 8 months) and costs. (LISA 72/2565)

No conclusions are offered in the notes, but the authors hope that librarians can apply the data to their own situations. (KK)

#115 **Indexing revisited** / B. Hawkins, B. Kelley, E. Mee and P. Scott – *New Library World* (ISSN 0307-4803), 80(948)June 1979, p.106-107.

Update of a survey of the coverage of periodicals by 3 indexing services: *Applied Science and Technology Index (ASTI), British Technology Index (BTI)*, and *Engineering Index (EI)* carried out in 1972 by students at Liverpool Polytechnic Department of Library and Information Studies. The services combined cover 2,087 periodical titles; *EI* covers 1,815; *BTI* 336; and *ASTI* 305. 23 journals are common to all 3 services. *EI*'s unique coverage extends to 1,475 titles; *BTI*'s-167 titles; and *ASTI*'s-99 titles. Overlap between *EI* and *BTI* is 163; *BTI/ASTI*-29; *ASTI/EI*-220; and all three-23. Statistics are given relating to coverage of individual papers within journals; and subscription rates are mentioned. (LISA 79/3582)

#116 **The information content of titles in engineering literature** / Robert T. Bottle – *IEEE Transactions on Engineering Writing and Speech* (ISSN 0018-9405), 13(2) September 1970, p.41-45.

A survey is made as to whether the title of an article conveys the content of the article by using previously indexed articles in *Applied Science and Technology Index (ASTI)*, *British Technology Index (BTI)*, *Engineering Index (EI)* and *Mass Spectrometry Bulletin*. Comparison is made of the indexing concept and keywords in the document titles as to whether they are identical, synonymous or neither. Results are produced from a study of 90 papers and a standard error is calculated on chemical and non-chemical articles. Some of the results suggest that putting the journal title as well as the document title into the computer would help searching. Using all possible synonyms instead of just one term considerably increased the amount retrieved. There is no obvious advantage in having *ASTI* when one already subscribes to *EI* and *BTI*. (LISA 70/2603)

The reason for the above conclusion is that the journal coverage of *EI* is superior to that of the other two and its abstracts are an additional advantage. Its depth of indexing, while better than that of *ASTI*, is not nearly so good as that of *BTI*. The main thing to be said against *BTI* is the national limitation to its journal coverage. (KK)

#117 **Municipal library notes** / E.A. Clough – *Library Association Record* (ISSN 0024-2195), 64(9) September 1962, p.333.

The author thinks it a pity that the Regional Library Bureaux were originally conceived and directed into the channels that made them become specialized cataloguing agencies rather than advanced inter-lending agencies. But the recent experience with the *British Technology Index* (BTI) gives an interesting example of what can be done. In the South West it was found that only 86 of the 400 periodicals covered by BTI remained outstanding after checking against a union catalogue published by the Library Association. Of these 86, 41 were found to be already taken by member libraries of the South-Western Regional Library System (SWRLS). The residue of 8 will certainly be dealt with by the libraries working together through the agency of SWRLS, etc. This implies that inter-library cooperation in this region will be advanced by making use of BTI. (KK)

#118 **A finding list of technical periodicals indexed in the British Technology Index and available through the libraries of the Yorkshire Regional Library System** / comp. William R. Flint and Margaret M. Flint for the Yorkshire Regional Library System – Sheffield, Central Library, 1963, 30p.

A list of journals indexed in the *British Technology Index* that are available through the libraries of the Yorkshire Regional Library System. (KK)

#119 The Institution of Mechanical Engineers: Council Minutes (Subject to confirmation) – London, Institution of Mechanical Engineers, February 1962, p.41-42.

Minutes 33-56 were presented at a meeting of the Council held on Wednesday, 28th February 1962 at 2.30 p.m. A meeting of the Publication and Library Committee held on 31st January1962 was reported by the Chairman, Sir Christopher Hinton, as Minute 42. It said that all Institution serial publications, i.e. Proceedings, Proceedings of the Automobile Division, "The Chartered Mechanical Engineer" and the "Journal of Mechanical Engineering Science" be presented regularly to the Library Association for indexing in a new bibliographical index entitled "British Technology Index." (KK)

#120 In brief [Flight technical articles indexed in BTI] – *Flight International* (ISSN 0015-3710), 93(3074)February 1968, p.199.

From the Library Association comes a note mentioning that the *British Technology Index* (a subject-guide to articles in British technical journals) includes references to *Flight* technical articles of page length or over. The index is published monthly (annual subscription £18 18s) by the Library Association at 7 Ridgmount Street, Store Street, London WC1. (Original text)

#121 [Radio Communication is not covered by BTI] – *New Library World* (ISSN 0307-4803), 73(864)June 1972, p.312.

Radio Communication is not listed in the journals covered by the *British Technology Index* (BTI). It is an important and scholarly publication, but its publishing body cannot afford to let BTI have free copies. Points out that there is a problem of the journal inclusion criterion in abstracting and indexing services. (KK)

#122 Management documentation services / Kenneth G.B. Bakewell – *Management Decision* (ISSN 0025-1747), 12(1)1974, p.65-74.

Emphasizes that this article is concerned with services providing 'information about management' rather than 'information for management'. The manager's need for information services is examined by reference to actual enquiries put by managers in their daily work. The present state of documentation services (e.g. books, periodicals, abstracting and indexing services, guides to research) is examined, together with the various kinds of libraries providing information services about management. Mentions that coverage of management journals by BTI and BHI is spasmodic, though they can occasionally be helpful. Finally, reasons for the non-use of existing services by managers are examined, and suggestions are made for the removal of these obstacles. (KK)

#123 **Scottish bibliography: past, present and future** / Ian R.M. Mowatt – *SLA News* (ISSN 0048-9786), (138) March-April 1977, p.245-249.

The *British National Bibliography* and British periodical indexes such as *British Humanities Index* and *British Technology Index* achieve only partial coverage of Scottish materials. This deficiency is partly remedied by the existence of a number of special, Scottish subject bibliographies. Several examples of these are mentioned, including: *Annual Bibliography of Scottish Literature*, the bibliographies in *Scottish Historical Review* and *Scottish Studies,* and *Recent Geographical Literature Relating to Scotland.* Considers the case for a Scottish bibliography which, to be useful, would need to list periodical articles and unpublished materials as well as monographs. Periodical coverage might be based on 130 core journals, plus a further 600 titles contributing the occasional relevant article. (LISA 77/3277)

20.30 Currency (Time-lag)

#124 **Quick indexes** – *Nature* (ISSN 0028-0836), 218(5142) May 1968, p.623-624. See also #275.

A survey of the *Nuclear Science Abstracts* and the *Physics Abstracts* reported in this journal showed that physicists have to wait on average just under 5 months for abstracts to appear after the publication of the original article (**Slow abstracts** – *Nature*, 216(5117) November 1967, p.737). To see how much quicker indexing journals, a *Nature* correspondent has made a survey of the time-lag in two journals: the *British Technology Index* (BTI) and the *Applied Science and Technology Index* (ASTI). The July 1967 issues were taken in each case. Just over 100 articles were taken at random from each journal. As expected, the results show that the two indexing journals are much quicker than the abstracting journals in bringing articles. *BTI* is considerably quicker than *ASTI*: its approximate mean date of publication is 7 weeks in comparison with *ASTI*'s 11 weeks. (KK)

#125(#124) **Indexing rates** – *Liaison* (no ISSN), October 1968, p.70.

Last November, *Nature* studied two abstract journals and showed that physicists have to wait on an average just under five months for abstracts to appear after the publication of the original paper. Recently, this was followed up with an examination of two indexing journals – *British technology index* and the American *Applied science and technology index*, published by H.W. Wilson. A hundred titles at random were taken from each journal (the July 1967 issues) and the time-lag in weeks charted. The survey showed that *BTI* had an approximate mean delay of seven weeks from publication and *ASTI*, one of eleven weeks. With the introduction of computerization, *BTI* is hoping to improve on this standard. (Original text)

20.40 Promotion and subscription rates

#126 **[Display of BTI]** – *Liaison* (no ISSN), July 1964, p.44 (includes a photograph).

The stand and display which was entered by The British Technology Index in the Research and Development Production Exhibition at Olympia early in May. (Original text)

#127 **British Technology Index: a subscriber's view** / *Sir* Harold Roxbee Cox – *New Scientist* (ISSN 0028-6664), 24(416)November 1964, p.390. See also class 80.40 Metal Box Ltd.

Chairman of the Metal Box Company Ltd, writes of his company's use of BTI as follows: "We find that its particular value lies not only in that it provide a key to articles in journals which we do not see as a matter of routine but also relieves us of the necessity to index in detail material marginal to our main interests appearing in some of the journals to which we do subscribe. In other words, we regard it as a good thing." The article is prepared by the Library Association, London. (KK)

#128 **Promotion** – *Annual report of the Council of the Association for the year ending 31st December, 1969: Presented at the annual meeting in London 1970* – London, Library Association, [1970], p.29.

For the first time, the Library Association exhibited at the American Library Association Convention and was able to introduce the Library Association's books and periodicals to a huge market which is very expensive to reach through the usual advertising channels. Since then, there has been a marked increase in North American sales and further promotion in this area is under consideration. Extensive promotion was undertaken on behalf of *Library and Information Science Abstracts* and *Journal of Librarianship* with satisfying results, and more limited advertising has had an effect on sales of *British Humanities Index* and *British Technology Index*. (Excerpt from original text)

#129 **Indexes up** – *Liaison* (no ISSN), January 1969, p.3.

Because of increased production costs, it has been decided that the subscription rates from January for *British technology index* shall be £22 10s. and for *British humanities index*, £14 14s. Both journals will then be moving over to A4 size and, for the second of the two, there will now be a fourth quarterly issue. (Original text)

20.50 Number of subscriptions

See also #262.

#130 **[Subscriptions to BTI]** – *Liaison* (no ISSN), July 1962, p.51.

Over 280 public libraries have now subscribed to the *British Technology Index*. With foreign and non-public library subscriptions the total now stands at 923. Surprisingly, there are about forty public libraries with populations of over 35,000 that have not subscribed. Up to May each monthly issue contained more material than its predecessors. (Original text)

#131 **British Technology Index** – *Library World* (ISSN 0024-2616), 64(745)July 1962, p.30.

Mentions that BTI is making slow but steady progress. Calls for public libraries' subscription to BTI. Argues that the smaller the library the more essential it was for BTI to be taken and that some larger libraries too could increase their orders. Points out that BTI's initial success needs the fullest possible support from the profession. Suggests those home librarians, who are still not subscribing might do well to ponder over the fact that nearly 40 per cent of BTI's subscribers are overseas libraries. (KK)

#132 **[Subscriptions to BTI]** – *Liaison* (no ISSN), November 1962, p.71.

Despite orders from the U.S.A. having fallen far short of their original estimate, the *British Technology Index* has reached its target of 1,000 subscriptions within eight months of first publication. (Original text)

#133 **Publications (iv) British Technology Index** – *Annual report of the Council of the Association for the year ending 31st December, 1962: Presented at the annual meeting in London 1963* – London, Library Association, [1963], p.12.

Publication of the *British Technology Index* commenced at the beginning of the year, and the monthly service was maintained according to plan. The *Index* had a generally favourable reception and circulation by the end of the year reached 1,025. This slightly exceeded the target figure envisaged in planning, but production and staff costs proved higher than estimated, with the result that the *Index* was not self-supporting by the end of the year. (Original text)

#134 **British Technology Index** – *Annual report of the Council of the Association for the year ending 31st December, 1963: Presented at the annual meeting in Birmingham 1964* – London, Library Association, [1964], p.17.

In its second year *British Technology Index* achieved approximately 10 per cent increase in subscriptions over the first year. The first annual volume appeared in July and sales of separate copies proved a useful addition to income. The publication was advertised extensively and the trend of subscriptions suggested that the project should be self-supporting in its third year. Currency of entries was maintained. Subscribers were still in process of discovering the use to which *British Technology Index* could be put and gave no clear indication of the direction in which they hoped the service might be extended. (Original text)

#135 **[British Technology Index]** / J.F.W.B. [John Frederick Walter Bryon] – *Library World* (ISSN 0024-2616), 65(760) October 1963, p.141-142.

Owing to the preceding failures of the Cleaver-Hume's three-part index and IOTA, there were those who prophesied woe for the *British Technology Index* (BTI). There is a sign of the need for technical information in industry and new technical colleges. At a recent LA Council meeting, the Publication Committee's recommendation that BTI should be regarded as a permanent part of LA's publishing programme was agreed *nem con*, despite it was not at that moment breaking even on costs. It was only a matter of time before subscriptions reached the breaking even point. Not only have the first year's subscriptions been maintained, but also new ones are coming in at an average rate of 15 per month. About two-fifths of the sales are overseas. There has been an initial reluctance on the part of a few industrial librarians. Many of their colleagues are finding BTI invaluable. Recommends colleagues in UK to subscribe to BTI at once. (KK)

#136 **[Subscriptions to BTI]** – *Liaison* (no ISSN), November 1963, p.79.

The target of 1,100 subscriptions for the *British Technology Index* for 1963 has now been exceeded, the Publication Committee reports. (Original text)

#137 **[Subscriptions to BTI]** – *Liaison* (no ISSN), August 1964, p.52.

The total of 1,231 subscriptions to *British Technology Index* have been received to date, an increase of 168 on the corresponding period for 1963, which, it is felt, makes the financial results for last year and the prospects for the current year very encouraging. The annual cumulative volume for 1963 is now available. (Original text)

#138 **British Technology Index** – *Annual report of the Council of the Association for the year ending 31st December, 1964: Presented at the annual meeting in Harrogate 1965* – London, Library Association, [1965], p.18.

There has been an increase in 14 per cent in subscriptions this year, and this should bring B.T.I. close to financial breakeven in respect of 1964 operations. Most of the increase has come from overseas. Growth of support at home is comparatively slow, and there are probably still 400 British firms with libraries which do not take B.T.I. (Original text)

#139 **B.T.I.** – *Liaison* (no ISSN), November 1964, p.68.

The article consists of remarks cited from D.E. Davinson's book entitled, "*Periodicals,*" revised edition, 1964. Remarks are largely concerned with public libraries which have not yet subscribed to BTI. (KK)

#140 **[Subscriptions to BTI]** – *Liaison* (no ISSN), July 1965, p.51.

Total sales for the full service of *British Technology Index* last year were 1,291 – an increase of 161 over the 1963 figures at the corresponding time. (Original text)

#141 **BTI surplus** – *Liaison* (no ISSN), August 1966, p.58. See also #189.

During 1965, and including the sales of annual volumes, *British Technology Index* showed a surplus of between £700 and £800. Arrangements with Rocappi Ltd. to undertake a pilot computer programme for the *Index* has been terminated, due to the firm's inability to offer a definite completion date. Discussion with other organizations are going on. (Original text)

#142 **Professional publishing in the UK: the literature of librarianship and information work, 1967-87** / Sheila Ritchie – *Journal of Librarianship* (ISSN 0022-2232), 22(1)January 1990, p.1-40.

In celebration of 20 years of publication of *Journal of Librarianship* the field of professional publishing of periodicals and monographs, in librarianship and information science, is reviewed for the period 1967-1987. Traces what was published, by whom, and for whom, at what prices and with what success. Tables are included covering: periodical titles existent in 1967; new periodical titles in the period 1968-1987; analysis of subscriptions to *British Technology Index*, for 1966 and 1967, by country, sales of Library Association (LA) book titles at 1970 with costs, income and 'profit'; LA overseas sales 1968, and the developments that have taken place in LISA, 1967-1987. (LISA 90/4818)

The breakdown of subscription to the LA's *British Technology Index* in June 1967 is shown in Table 3 (1,380 in total from the Editor's report). By June 1968 the total had risen to 1,437 and by January 1969 to 1,517. The Editor of *BTI* had been so diligent and accurate in recording his subscriptions, but reported mournfully that he could not say what the sales breakdown was for 1969 as he had not got any figures from the Book Centre that began to stock and distribute books and journals for LA. (KK)

20.60 Change of size

See also #129, #144 and #206.

#143 **BTI and BHI** – *Liaison* (no ISSN), October 1968, p.70.

The international A4 size is to be adopted for *British technology index*, and *British humanities index* from the beginning of next year and for *British education index* for the volume for 1970-71. (Excerpt from original text)

20.70 Use of magnetic tape

See also #202, #204, #205 and #285.

#144 **Other periodical publications** – *Annual report of the Council of the Association for the year ending 31st December, 1968: Presented at the annual meeting in London 1969* – London, Library Association, [1969], p.26.

Plans are in hand for *British Technology Index*, *British Humanities Index* and *British Education Index* to be computer typeset, and all are changing to A4 size. The Editor of *British Technology Index* is investigating the possibility of using magnetic tape, produced in the course of computer typesetting, to provide selections and rearrangements of Index material in computer print-out form to meet individual subscribers' needs. (Excerpt from original text)

#145 **British Technology Index** – *Aslib Proceedings* (ISSN 0001-253X), 23(5) May 1971, p.220.

Says that the *British Technology Index* (BTI) is now available in the form of industry compatible 7-track magnetic tape that is obtainable in advance of the printed publication. The tape data contains the usual markers to facilitate rearrangement by author, title, or source journal. A full specification may be obtained from the BTI Editorial Office, Argyle House, 29 Euston Road, London NW1 2SS (phone: 01-8373222), UK. (KK)

20.80 Microfiche form

#146 **Into microfiche** – *Liaison* (no ISSN), October 1970, p.62.

An agreement has been reached with World Microfilms to publish back issues of the *British humanities index* and the *British technology index* in microfiche form. These are now available in the autumn list, covering all back issues, and World Microfilms, who operate from 48a Goodge Street, London W1, propose to promote them to all major libraries in the world. At the same time, conventional copies of all back issues of the journals are still available from the Publication Department. After this publication of all the existing back issues, the Company will continue to reproduce each year's issues in microfiche, following the completion of the volume for any given year. (Original text)

20.90 Others

#147 **Effects of the postal strike** – *Liaison* (no ISSN), April 1971, p.25.

Stories of the postal strike are still being "swapped," like stories about one's own bomb during the Blitz, and the Association was one of the bodies which suffered quite heavily as a result of it. Overseas copies of *British technology index* were distributed by being sent to Amsterdam for posting and the printers delivered quite a large number of those in the Birmingham area. (Excerpt from original text)

#148 **BTI "blacking" threat** – *Liaison* (no ISSN), June 1972, p.50.

Production of the *British Technology Index* (BTI) was recently threatened by a decision of the National Graphical Association (NGA) to "black" its copy unless the two members of staff, who punch tape for production by computer, were members of NGA. (KK)

30 INDEXING SYSTEM

30.10 General description

For a thorough study of BTI indexing system, the following items that are almost written by Coates and largely classified in 20.10 General description of BTI and 40.30 Computerization of BTI should also be looked through.

#104 British Technology Index (E.J. Coates, 1962).

#105 Monitoring current technical information with the British Technology Index (E.J. Coates, 1962).

#106 Aims and methods of the British Technology Index (E.J. Coates, 1963).

#108 Introduction [British Technology Index. Annual volume 1962] (E.J. Coates, 1963).

#112 British Technology Index (E.J. Coates, 1970).

#208 British Technology Index – a study of the application of computer processing to index production (E.J. Coates and I. Nicholson, 1967).

#214 A project to study the feasibility of the production of the British Technology Index by computer. Final report May 1968 (I. Nicholson, 1968).

#216 The computerisation of the British Technology Index (E.J. Coates, 1968).

#220 Computerisation of British Technology Index: man-machine collaboration in the production of indexes (E.J. Coates, 1968).

#224 Computer assistance in the production of BTI (E.J. Coates, 1968).

#225 Computerised data processing for British Technology Index (E.J. Coates, 1969).

#297 Computer handling of social science terms and their relationships (E.J. Coates, 1969).

#149 **Scientific and technical indexing** / E.J. Coates – *Indexer* (ISSN 0019-4131), 5(1) Spring 1966, p.27-34. Reprinted in: *Training in indexing: a course of the Society of Indexers* / ed. G. Norman Knight – Cambridge, MA, M.I.T. Press, 1969, p.128-141. The book was translated into Japanese as: *Sakuin: sakusei no riron to jissai* / tr. Yukio Fujino – Tokyo, Nichigai Associates, 1981, 232p. (ISBN 4-8169-0051-9), and Coates' paper was translated as: **Kagaku gijutsu no sakuin sakusei** (p.137-150). The original English paper was further reprinted in: *Indexers on indexing: a selection of articles published in The Indexer* / ed. Leonard Montague Harrod for the Society of Indexers – New York, Bowker, 1978, p.219-225. (ISBN 0-8352-1099-5). See also #236.

The indexing of scientific and technical literature is not fundamentally different from other kinds of indexing. The author distinguishes three main levels of indexing. At the lowest level the words of the text or title are just manipulated into alphabetical order, e.g. KWIC indexing. At this level indexing can be performed quickly and cheaply but inadequately. At the second level the indexer attempts to identify synonyms or phrases of equivalent meaning and either list all references under both terms or under one with a reference from the other. In compiling a large index, classification of the terms is the only certain way of finding all the possible synonyms. At the third level the indexer attempts to relate terms to other terms with a wider meaning. Classification of the terms is necessary again to identify these inclusion relationships. Various methods of arranging the terms in an index entry, including the method used in *British Technology Index*, and the problems associated with them are discussed. (LSA 66/558)

#150(#149)   **[Review of] Training in indexing: a course of the Society of Indexers** / Michael Gorman – *Journal of Documentation* (ISSN 0022-0418), 25(3) September 1969, p.273-274. See also #180 and #236.

The book is made up of a series of lectures delivered by experts in indexing at courses sponsored by the Society of Indexers. Each lecture deals with a particular aspect of indexing books and periodicals. Many indexers have had to learn by experience, by trial and error. The Society of Indexers have tried to remedy this situation by holding courses and discussion meetings. The usefulness of the book is that the list of authors is formidable and each of the persons is a noted in his field. In a chapter "Scientific and technical indexing," E.J. Coates outlines the general principle of subject indexing, with special reference to scientific works. He deals with a difficult subject in remarkably concise and lucid manner. (KK)

#151(#149)   **[Review of] Indexers on indexing: a selection of articles published in The Indexer** / V. de P. Roper – *Journal of Documentation* (ISSN 0022-0418), 37(1) March 1981, p.51-52. See also #106, #153, #183, #185, #225 and #248.

The book is the 21st anniversary publication to mark the establishment of the Society of Indexers. Many of the articles are standard items in their own subject area. The 59 articles reprinted from issues of *The Indexer* have been carefully chosen and grouped together into subject sections. Mentions that it was particularly good to see the four papers by Coates chosen for inclusion and that each is still leading in its subject field. Adds that two of these articles are related to the *British Technology Index* and are taken with a third by Singleton on the same topic. (KK)

#152(#149)   **The Indexer thirty years ago – continued** / Hazel K. Bell – *Indexer* (ISSN 0019-4131), 20(1) April 1996, p.23.

E.J. Coates, editor of the *British Technology Index*, in 'Scientific and technical indexing,' compares scientific literature which 'contains greater number of concepts *in toto* and a far higher proportion of precisely defined concepts than does the literature of the humanities ... from the point of view of the battle between words and meanings, the scientific indexer gets off relatively lightly' (soft texts paid due regard again!). (Excerpt from original text)

#153   **Technical indexing at B.T.I.** / Alan Singleton – *Indexer* (ISSN 0019-4131), 9(2)

October 1974, p.37-49. Reprinted in: *Indexers on indexing: a selection of articles published in The Indexer* / ed. Leonard Montague Harrod for the Society of Indexers – New York, Bowker, 1978, p.247-259. (ISBN 0-8352-1099-5). See also #151.

The author worked for 6 months as an indexer on BTI and here presents his personal view of the service. Emphasises the debt owed to Ranganathan's ideas of synthesis, facet analysis and chain indexing. Although an analytically derived index, BTI has an authority file and many points of similarity with the thesaurus of coordinate indexing. Considers the use of the computer for typesetting and as an aid to compilation. Explains some difficulties likely to be experienced by users, e.g., the heading LASERS : Machining can be a little confusing, in the hope that these may then be overcome. Presents a brief analysis of 6 months of a BTI indexer's time. (LISA 74/3761)

#154 (#153) A comment on "Technical indexing at BTI." / E.J. Coates – *Indexer* (ISSN 0019-4131), 9(2) October 1974, p.50-52.

The editor of BTI agrees with much of what is put forward in [LISA abstract] 74/3761. Describes the essential difference between relational and facet analysis, although both are ways of describing the same situation, and deals with BTI's use of chain indexing and its modification for the production of cross references. The change advocated for the Agent/Action structure (LASERS : Machining) would result in some loss of useful collocation although it is conceded that several people have queried this particular construction. Considers the detailed breakdown of a beginner indexer's first 6 months a useful addition to an area of very scanty information but feels certain that the second 6 months would show a regularity of tasks which the 1st period, as untypical, would not. (LISA 74/3762)

#155 (#153, #154) The Indexer thirty years ago / Hazel K. Bell – *Indexer* (ISSN 0019-4131), 24(2) October 2004, p.104-105 (esp. p.104).

The October 1974 issue of *The Indexer*, Volume 9, No.2, consisted of 56 pages, strongly featuring technology. It opened with 13 pages by Alan Singleton on 'Technical indexing at *B.T.I.*,' the abstract explaining 'This is a description and personal view of the *British Technology Index*. ... Some difficulties that users are likely to experience are explained. ... Some suggestions for further development are made.' ... This was followed by 'A comment on "Technical indexing at *B.T.I.*"' by E.J. Coates, *B.T.I.*'s editor. He points out that Singleton spent only six months working as an indexer there, observing with a certain stiffness, ... 'though I am not sure what general conclusions can be drawn from it.' (Excerpt from original text)

#156 British Technology Index (Coates) [In German] / Reinhard Supper – In his: *Neuere Methoden der intellektuellen Indexierung: britische Systeme unter besonderer Berucksichtigung von PRECIS* – Munchen, Verlag Dokumentation Saur, 1978, p.89-100, and 198. (Beitrage zur Informations- und Dokumentationswissenschaft, Folge 11) (ISBN 3-7940-

3721-9).

The focus of this book lies on the critical description of Austin's *PREserved Context Index System* (PRECIS). Other indexing systems of UK treated in the book are: Farradane's *Relational Indexing*; Coates' *British Technology Index* (BTI); and Lynch's *Articulated Subject Index*. BTI is introduced with such features as: coverage; currency; subject headings; inversion cross-references produced by chain procedure; and the scale of organization, i.e. small staff. Mention is made of the necessity for computerization and of the tasks that the computer took the place of. Relational analysis that is central to BTI indexing system is considered, together with punctuation marks introduced on the occasion of computerization. The final section discusses comments on BTI that are concerned with both advantages and disadvantages. (Ika Mantani)

30.20 Relational analysis and citation order

See also #297.

#157 **The analysis of phrases** / B.C. Vickery – In his: *Classification and indexing in science*, 3rd ed. – London, Butterworths, 1975, p.101-103. (ISBN 0-408-70662-7).

Describes Cutter's rules which were concerned with specific entry. Sums up that Cutter recognized three types of phrase that might be inverted: (1) the noun preceded by an adjective, such as 'Agricultural Chemistry'; (2) the noun preceded by an adjective noun, such as 'Death Penalty'; and (3) the prepositional phrase, such as 'Fertilization of Flowers'. Cutter discussed three possible rules: (a) not invert, (b) invert only type, and (c) invert any type of compound name, i.e. the most significant word of the phrase. Coates has intensively analyzed adjective phrases according to the semantic categories of their components, and applied his principles in the construction of the *British Technology Index* (BTI). He recognizes four semantic categories: Thing, Material, Action and Property. Other words in phrases may represent the type or purpose of thing, material, action or property. A dozen kinds of compound name are derived from binary combinations of categories, and a rule as to the inversion of each is put forward by Coates. When not inverted, the colon as a separation is introduced between the words in the phrase, and the phrase becomes a heading and subheading. A further step is to develop rules for compounds of more than two words. Concludes that the grouping found in BTI is controlled in a way that is completely analogous to the principles used in faceted classification. (KK)

#158 **British Technology Index** / K.G.B. Bakewell – In his: *A manual of cataloguing practice* – Oxford, Pergamon Press, 1972, p.231-232, 97-98, and 271-272. (International series of monographs in library and information science, 14) (ISBN 0-08-016697-0). See also #295.

Coates developed Kaiser's 'Thing-Process' breakdown into a more precise formula for the *British Technology Index*, distinguishing between properties, actions, materials, and parts of a thing or entity. Originally all relations were introduced by a comma, but a further development in 1968, associated with the use of a computer for the generation of cross-references, was the introduction of two other punctuation symbols, the colon and the semicolon. Coates distinguishes between *syntactic* relations (relations subsisting between the property, action, material or part on the one hand, and the thing or entity on the other) and *generic* relations (those which define or delimit a thing or entity). Syntactic relations are introduced by a colon, generic relations by a comma except in the case of a material, when a semicolon is used. Examples belonging to either of the two basic relations in BTI are given, together with those of cross-references generated from a subject heading. Introduces the use of BTI principles for the production of the subject catalogue at the library of the Natural Rubber Producers' Research Association. (KK)

#159 **Some properties of relationships in the structure of indexing languages** / E.J. Coates – *Journal of Documentation* (ISSN 0022-0418), 29(4) December 1973, p.390-404.

Relational analysis as an alternative to the 'categorical' view of syntactic structures in indexing is discussed. Relational categorisation of syntactic structures by reference to the meaning of the spaces between constituent terms may point the way to classification structures which are stable to new knowledge and discipline independent. General properties of syntactic strings, logical articulation, disarticulation, and linearisation of branching relationships are discussed, together with the role of relational symbolism in significant-word based searches. Derivative relations which arise out of an inclusion relation between an isolated concept and the relation-linked combination of which it forms a part are outlined. (LISA 74/540)

#160 **[Review]** / E.J. Coates – *Journal of Documentation* (ISSN 0022-0418), 32(1) March 1976, p.85-96. The following is reviewed:

  PRECIS: a manual of concept analysis and subject indexing / Derek Austin – London, Council of the British National Bibliography, 1974, 551p. (ISBN 0-900220-42-2).

The 12-page review of the PRECIS manual includes comparison with BTI indexing system at some points. Argues that the handling of prepositional relationships in PRECIS is to an unacceptable extent arbitrary and too dependent on linguistic accidents. The experiment of bibliographical output strings probably passes muster to the extent that users manage to interpret the Qualifier as 'difference specifiers' of the Lead. Concludes that the chief weakness of PRECIS is at the point at which it may justly claim to have been most original, i.e. the matter of 'differencing operators.' (KK)

#161 **Classification in information retrieval: the twenty years following Dorking** / E.J. Coates – *Journal of Documentation* (ISSN 0022-0418), 34(4) December 1978, p.288-299. Reprinted in: *From classification to "Knowledge organization": Dorking revisited or "Past* *is prelude"* / ed. Alan Gilchrist – The Hague, FID, 1997, p.11-20. (FID occasional paper, 14) (ISBN 92-66-00714-5).

Paper contributed to a memorial issue for Herbert Coblans (1906-77) who has encouraged the author to carry out his works since early in the 1960s. Describes that the Dorking conference in 1957 caused a further breakthrough in understanding of classification at a fundamental level comparable to that achieved earlier by Ranganathan. Implementation has mainly been concerned with catching up with the theory. But practice has not overtaken theory as there has been little theory to overtake. Since 1957 progress on the theoretical side of classification has been exclusively in relation to the syntactic axis. On the semantic side there has been little progress. The most important realization in the syntactic refinement process has been that facets are functions or superficial manifestations of relations between concepts. As to general subject indexing system, there were three relation-based systems: *British Technology Index; Articulated Subject Index* (ASI); and PRECIS. ASI is unique in that relation identification process is carried out at the verbal level, i.e. 'prepositions'. The 'Differencing operators' of PRECIS are used in handling of many kinds of adjective+noun or noun+noun phrases. But there is a danger that any syntactic string could be interpreted as 'difference relations' which should be associated with semantic axis. Points out that classification for information retrieval is obsolete or of dubious utility have come from two quarters: mechanization and system evaluation. (KK)

#162 **The role of classification in information retrieval: action and thought in the contribution of Brian Vickery** / E.J. Coates – *Journal of Documentation* (ISSN 0022-0418), 44(3)September 1988, p.216-225. Reprinted in: *Facets of knowledge organization: Proceedings of the ISKO UK Second Biennial Conference, 4th-5th July 2011, London* / ed. Alan Gilchrist and Judi Vernau – Bingley, Emerald, 2012, p.191-202. (ISBN 978-1-78052-614-0).

An assessment of Vickery's contribution to the development of classification for retrieval. On the practical side his work in the early years of the Classification Research Group and elsewhere enhanced the status of classification for retrieval as a significant field of study. On the intellectual side he demonstrated the use of his own elaborated version of Ranganathan's facets for the purposes of western special libraries. Discusses some remaining 'grey areas' in faceted classification, classificatory fragments implicit in many thesauri, and the value for expository purposes of a mildly polemic approach to issues in classification. In the later part of the paper points out that Vickery notices that facets may be characterized alternatively as categories of concepts or as a class of relationships between concepts. Facet category captions are sometimes denoting phenomena (e.g. Energy, Matter) and sometimes relationships between such phenomena (e.g. Part, Type, Agent, Patient). Argues that facet relational labels need not include any which denote phenomena, and that facets are more unambiguously presented in relational terms for Vickery's expository purposes. (KK)

#163 **Relational systems in indexing and classification: a study of conceptual relations necessary for information retrieval** [In Japanese] / Keiichi Kawamura – *Journal of Japan Society of Library and Information Science* (ISSN 1344-8668), 48(2)June 2002, p.73-93.

Both facet analysis and relational analysis are methods of subject analysis in the European tradition. The former is based on categorization of the terms themselves and the latter analyzes the meaning of the spaces between terms in syntactic structures in indexing. The purpose of this paper is to find a satisfactory solution to the problem of how many relations are, in principle, necessary for information retrieval. Nine relational systems (Farradane's Relational Indexing, Perry/Kent's WRU system, Kervegant's supplementary system for UDC, Leroy/Braffort's system for CEA, Gardin's SYNTOL, Coates' BTI, Lynch's ASI, Austin's PRECIS and Coates' BSO) were surveyed and an inventory was made of the relations used in these nine systems, which amounted to 170 in all. Based upon the assumption that the nine systems as a whole cover the necessary relations, the author proposes that a comparison of these relations should be made at concept level by making use of a fully faceted general classification, and expects that the most suitable scheme for the comparison will be BSO whose structure lays stress on facet relations rather than facet categories. (Original abstract)

30.30 Handling of compound terms

#164 **[Analysis of compound terms]** / Alan Gilchrist – In his: *The thesaurus in retrieval* – London, Aslib, 1971, p.44. (ISBN 0-8514-2036-2).

Says that Coates' book *Subject catalogues* contains a great deal of useful material on the structure of compound terms. He is editor of the *British Technology Index* and his main interest has been to establish rules for the most helpful order in which compounds should be entered. This will be of use to the compilers of thesauri who allow inverted entry for compounds. The method used by Coates is to amplify a compound into a phrase by reinstating the missing prepositions, at which stage it becomes easier to make a logical decision as to whether to invert or not. Thus *bicycle wheel* is amplified to 'wheel of bicycle' and the subsequent subject heading becomes 'BICYCLES, Wheels', which reverses the order found in the amplification; but *resistance welding* becomes 'welding by (exploiting electrical) resistance' (Property of metals) and the preferred subject heading is 'WELDING, Resistance' which agrees with the amplified order. Most thesauri favour direct entry for all compounds, and in this case the value of Coates' approach is as an aid towards the better understanding of the structure of compounds. (KK)

#165 **Compound words: a problem in post-coordinate retrieval systems** / Kevin P. Jones – *Journal of the American Society for Information Science* (ISSN 0002-8231), 22(4) July-August 1971, p.242-250. See also #295.

The problem of compound words has become evident in post-coordinate indexing systems. If too many words are fractured, or the wrong categories are chosen for fracturing, there is a low retrieval performance. Rules for handling compound words, including those for pre-coordinate or rotated indexes are discussed in detail, including rules made up by Cutter, Farradane, *British Technology Index*, Taube, Engineering Joint Council and Jespersen. Syntactic origins are also explored, pointing out different types of compound words, e.g. abbreviated statements from longer phrases. These considerations have been combined to produce a set of rules employed at the Natural Rubber Producers' Research Association. In use for 2 years, they have been of great assistance in decision-making and rectifying earlier decisions, thus making the vocabulary more consistent. (LISA 71/2094)

#166 **Problems associated with the use of compound words in thesauri, with special reference to BS 5723: 1979** / Kevin P. Jones – *Journal of Documentation* (ISSN 0022-0418), 37(2)June 1981, p.53-68.

Word compounding is the practice of putting words, or parts of words, together to form new words. Former attempts to devise rules which attempt to approach the problem via syntax were not altogether satisfactory. Proposes that the major criteria for handling compound words should rest upon their orthography, lexicography and semantics, with special attention to the possible occurrence of homographs. Suggestions contained in *"British Standard 5723 – Guidelines for the establishment and development of monolingual thesauri"* are assessed in relation to these criteria. The standard is criticized for its insufficient attention to mechanized systems' requirements and partial failure in not recording the divergent needs of pre- and post-coordinate systems. Coates' rules which were presented in the 1960 book and were later put into practice in the *British Technology Index* are introduced in full. These rules are based on the analysis of relationship of prepositional phrases. (KK)

#167 **The handling of compound terms in indexing systems** / T.N. Rajan – *Journal of Library and Information Science* (ISSN 0970-714X), 1(2)December 1976, p.169-190.

The handling of compound terms has been one of the oldest problems in alphabetical indexing. A compound term is defined as a unit concept represented by two or more words, of which only one is the focus and the rest of word(s) is/are either a qualifier(s) to the focus or qualifier(s) to the qualifier(s). Not only have pre-coordinate indexing systems been confronted with this problem, but also post-coordinate systems have been necessitated to tackle it. Describes the handling of compound terms in three major pre-coordinate indexing systems: POPSI, BTI and PRECIS. Makes a comparative assessment of their approaches to the problem. Suggests that a classificatory approach would perhaps be more helpful than a linguistic one. (KK)

30.40 Vocabulary control

#168 **Control of vocabulary in a current awareness service** / E.J. Coates – In: *Proceedings of Small Meeting of Czechoslovak and British Information Specialists, Liblice, May 16-21, 1966* – Prague, Centre for Scientific, Technical and Economic Information, 1967, p.68-74.

Vocabulary control is defined as the process of converting natural language terms into index language terms, including syntactical problems in precoordinated index systems. Descriptor lists are customarily updated by a delayed referral procedure, but this is not appropriate to a current awareness index service, which must establish new terms at the time of initial indexing. The experience of the *British Technology Index* in this connection is described, and the importance of classificatory procedures and relational analysis between concepts is stressed. The bearing of index specificity on vocabulary control is also briefly discussed. (Original abstract)

#169 **[Review]** / Philip R.D. Corrigan – *Journal of Documentation* (ISSN 0022-0418), 21(1) March 1965, p.70-73. The following is reviewed:
British Humanities Index. Annual volume 1963 – London, Library Association, 1964, 618p.

BHI is a subject and author index to over 300 periodicals. Says that one could give BHI loud and prolonged applause, but that this cannot be done. Points out that the errors are of two kinds: errors at the indexing stage and errors at the proof-reading stage. Describes a short test and question in the field of education chosen. The predominant fault with the indexing of BHI is a very poor state of control of vocabulary. The second fault is a lack of consistency in subject analysis. As a remedy for these faults, recommends a thorough overhaul of the indexing vocabulary, using techniques suggested by Coates in his book on subject catalogues and his writings about BTI. Concludes that the errors above-mentioned will be eradicated only by allying the natural language to the 'automatic memory' of a classificatory structure. (KK)

#170(#169) **[New editor of BHI was formerly chief indexer of BTI]** – *Liaison* (no ISSN), November 1967, p.86. See also #180.

The editorship of *British Humanities Index* has now been taken over by Mrs. B.M. Mason, in succession to Mr. Peter Ferriday, who resigned to take up a lectureship at Manchester. Mrs. Mason was formerly chief indexer with *British Technology Index*. (Original text)

30.50 Chain procedure for generating cross-references from subject headings

See also #19, #36, #37, #38 and #41.

#171 Chain procedure: application in the British Technology Index / E.J. Coates – *Electro-technology* (ISSN 0013-4643), 8(Special documentation issue), January-February 1964, p.33-39.

Describes the Chain Procedure as an alternative to arbitrarily limited permutation of index components. Its economy is discussed together with the problem of unsought headings and the need to exclude Genus-Species pairs from qualifying terms. Discusses its role and limitations in drawing attention to distributed relatives. Explains its adaptation for alphabetical subject catalogue and for the construction of subject headings for *British Technology Index*. (Original abstract)

#172 Documentation of the spiral library service / S.R. Ranganathan – *IASLIC Bulletin* (ISSN 0018-8441), 8(4)December 1963, p.180-210.

Presidential address presented at the 5th Conference of the Indian Association of Special Libraries and Information Centres (IASLIC), University of Poona, 21-24 October 1963. Describes the development of library services to meet the growing needs of the community. A brief survey is made of experiments taking place throughout the world in classification, indexing, and the use of machines in abstracting and information retrieval. Special mention is made of the *British National Bibliography* (BNB) and the *British Technology Index* (BTI). Points out that in the use of chain procedure outside India, UK has gained considerable experience on a large scale in BNB. A recent experimental use of chain procedure in the dictionary form is BTI. The Editor of BTI wrote to Ranganathan in a letter dated 31 July 1963, "You will see some of your own ideas, not I think too heavily disguised or mutilated." The Editor has stated that the rules of chain procedure can be framed to produce any desired alphabetical arrangement of multiple subject headings. Says that BTI is a challenge to a young aspirant to formulate the rules of chain procedure implied in its subject headings. (KK)

#173 British Technology Index / John Metcalfe – In his: *Alphabetical subject indication of information* – New Brunswick, NJ, Graduate School of Library Science, Rutgers State University, 1965, p.83-89. (Rutgers series on systems for the intellectual organization of information, 3).

Discussion is largely focused on chain procedure that is adopted by the *British Technology Index* (BTI). Enumerates many points of BTI's cross-references, which are regarded by the author as weakness of chain procedure. There are sometimes comparisons of cross-references between BTI and the *Applied Science and Technology Index*. (KK)

#174(#173) [Review of] Alphabetical subject indication of information / E.J. Coates – *Journal of Documentation* (ISSN 0022-0418), 22(1)March 1966, p.61-63.

Mentions that in 1964 the Council on Library of Congress (LC) issued a report prepared by L.F. Buckland called "The recording of Library of Congress bibliographical data in

#175   30.50 Chain procedure for generating cross-references from subject headings   #177

machine form." The report felt a lot of essential problems to be solved. Argues that anyone hoping to find answer, or even a clue to answer, to the problems in the book under review is likely to be disappointed. Because a large part of the book is taken up by a defense of the intuitive working procedures which underlie conventional subject cataloguing of LC type. Admits that the book has a useful chapter on the history of subject cataloguing since the late 18th century, but that the most recent item in this developmental series, the chain procedure of Ranganathan and its modifications is anathema to Metcalfe. Makes a detailed comparison between chain procedure and Metcalfe's system of subject heading with one subheading, i.e. Object and Aspect formula. (KK)

#175(#173)   **[Review of] Alphabetical subject indication of information** / Jack Mills – *Library Resources & Technical Services* (ISSN 0024-2527), 10(4)Fall 1966, p.527-529.

Mentions that Metcalfe discusses three main methods of pre-coordinating a compound: (1) single entry under a coextensive heading, supplemented by references from each of the distributed relatives – the *British Technology Index* is an exceptional and prominent example; (2) multiple entry with coextensive heading permuted to give different citation order – the classified file – UDC; and (3) multiple entry, with non-specific headings – the form favoured by most American A/Z catalogs and by Metcalfe. There exists the problem of "citation order" of the elements in a subject headings, but Metcalfe implies to dismiss the important problem saying, "unnecessary difficulty seems to be introduced." He describes the A/Z catalog as "known names and known order," which the reviewer regards as somewhat deceptive. Points out Metcalfe's looseness of thinking and inaccuracy of observation mainly concerning Coates' theory of subject catalogues and chain procedure. (KK)

#176   **John Metcalfe and the subject catalogue** / R.K. Olding – *Australian Library Journal* (ISSN 0004-9670), 20(4)May 1971, p.13-16.

There is some doubt, internationally, on whether Metcalfe should be listed in the annals of fame or infamy. He views subject work as *indication*, not education and rejects the theories of Richardson, Bliss and Ranganathan. With Kaiser, Metcalfe's development of Cutter's treatment of complex subjects is a major advance; it clashes seriously with chain procedure as exemplified in the *British Technology Index*. Metcalfe should be lauded and thanked for long researches, identification with problems, pungent criticisms, interest in teaching the subject and insistence that cataloguing is an art, not a science. (LISA 71/1670)

#177   **British Technology Index** / C.P. Auger – *Library Association Record* (ISSN 0024-2195), 71(8)August 1969, p.260.

Once again the annual volume of *British technology index* has landed on my desk, and once again I am not sure whether to cheer or to cry. I am delighted to have at my finger-tips a key to material contained in British technical journals, but I am daunted by the vast areas of "see" references (for example, page 419, "Flow"; and page 887, "Reinforced"). Is there any chance of diverting some of the effort at present applied in cross-referencing to the compilation of an author index? It would make the work so much more useful. (Original text)

#178(#177) **British Technology Index** / E.J. Coates – *Library Association Record* (ISSN 0024-2195), 71(8) August 1969, p.260.

Replies that many people will share Auger's view that BTI should have an author index. Admits that the provision of an author index will be regarded as first priority when the author is in position of expanding the present service. But refuses to try to free resources for producing an author index by cutting back the existing subject index. Points out that Auger's ambivalent feelings correspond to the occupational dilemma of indexers. Declares that he does choose the risk of daunting the user by the vast areas of "see references" rather than the risk of deleting useful lead-in points caused by the mere simplicity in appearance. (KK)

#179 **[Review]** / K.G.B. Bakewell – *Indexer* (ISSN 0019-4131), 11(4) October 1979, p.244-246. The following is reviewed:

Indexing concepts and methods / Harold Borko and Charles L. Bernier – New York, Academic Press, 1978, 261p. (ISBN 0-12-118660-1).

The aim of the book is to 'provide a basis for a well-balanced course of instruction in indexing.' But such a work as this which completely ignores 'chain indexing' must be of very limited value for courses in indexing in British library schools. Points out that a bibliography in the book includes such notable British names as Aitchison, Austin, Cleverdon, Gilchrist, Knight, McColvin and Sparck-Jones but omits two major British writers on 'chain indexing', Coates and Mills, and also the originator of the technique, Ranganathan. Emphasizes that no chapter on computer-aided indexing can be complete without any reference to the *British Technology Index*. (KK)

30.60 References made to BTI with other systems

#180 **Indexing of periodicals** / Peter Ferriday – *Indexer* (ISSN 0019-4131), 4(2) Autumn 1964, p.34-38, and 50. Reprinted with the addition of first eleven paragraphs by the editor in: *Training in indexing: a course of the Society of Indexers* / ed. G. Norman Knight – Cambridge, MA, M.I.T. Press, 1969, p.96-108. The book was translated into Japanese as: *Sakuin: sakusei no riron to jissai* / tr. Yukio Fujino – Tokyo, Nichigai Associates, 1981, 232p. (ISBN 4-8169-0051-9), and Ferriday's paper was translated as: **Teiki kankobutsu no sakuin** (p.105-118). See also #150 and #170.

After considering two pioneering indexes the *Gentleman's Magazine* 1787-1818, 2 vols. 1821, and *Notes and Queries*, Vols. 1-12, 1856, some current indexes are examined with the idea of determining their effectiveness and possible improvements. There are the indexes to *Public Administration, Church Quarterly Review, Adult Education, Burlington Magazine, The Listener, Discovery, The Modern Language Review, Nature*, and the *Journal* of the Royal Society of Arts. Concludes that 'the required development would seem in the direction of subject indexing as used in the *British Technology Index*, and the abandonment of the chance involved in such notions as "significant words" and "keywords"'. (LSA 64/14860)

#181 **Indexing and abstracting serials: some recent developments** / Derek Fielding – *Australian Library Journal* (ISSN 0004-9670), 14(1)March 1965, p.27-28. See also #72 and #73.

There have been interesting developments in the indexing, and in the arrangement of, serial abstracting and indexing services for last five years. The narrow and arid traditional arguments of alphabetico versus classified are reviewed in the light of computer facilities which ease the burden of clerical works and make possible activities which were previously beyond consideration. Publications referred to are: *Physics Abstracts, Electrical Engineering Abstracts, British Technology Index (BTI), Index Medicus, Biological Abstracts, Chemical Abstracts* and *Engineering Index*. Points out that the last pre-computer innovation in entry arrangement is to be found in BTI. Explains the principle of entry arrangement in BTI by referring to Coates' ideas, together with Lewis' claims that BTI is either an alphabetico-classed or a classification of technical articles. Emphasizes that whatever hybrid BTI is, it certainly does not produce entries under simple headings. (KK)

#182 **Two steps forward ...** / Derek Austin – In: *Itself an education (Six lectures on classification)*, 2nd edition containing a continuation by Derek Austin entitled "*Two steps forward ...*" / Bernard I. Palmer – London, Library Association, 1971, p.69-111. (SBN 85365-434-4).

Part 1 (p.7-67) consists of 6 lectures given by Palmer in Oslo and Copenhagen, in Winter 1961. Part 2 (p.69-111), by Austin, extends the 1st edition with a long essay that shows the ways in which the views of classification theorists have been modified during the 10 years, especially the introduction of computer. Part 2 discusses: classification for shelf ordering and indexing; subject indexing and concept organisation; the Aslib-Cranfield experiments; 'hard' and 'soft' subject fields; chain indexing in the *British National Bibliography* and the *British Technology Index* (BTI); Farradane's relational indexing; Lynch's Articulated Subject Index; and PRECIS. Points out that the PMEST formula of Ranganathan has proved to be an invaluable decision-making tool independent of any notated schedules, and that the first public demonstration of a logically structured pre-coordinated index divorced from the tables of a classification scheme came with the publication of BTI. (KK)

#182a(#182) **[Review of] Itself an education (Six lectures on classification), 2nd edition containing a continuation by Derek Austin entitled "Two steps forward**

..." / John Metcalfe – *Australian Library Journal* (ISSN 0004-9670), 20(11)December 1971, p.39.

Says that there is not a continuation but a contradiction between Palmer's 1961 lectures and Austin's essay. The latter is more original and important than the former which followed the line of the 1955 manifesto of CRG: The need for a faceted classification as the basis of all methods of information retrieval. Argues that one of Austin's steps forward is to distinguish broad shelf classification from theories of synthetic classification for minute document specification, and that the other is to assert that there can be logically structured pre-coordinated indexing not derived from any classification, such as PRECIS. Points out that Austin says that Coates first publicly demonstrated this structured indexing in his BTI in 1962, but that Kaiser was earlier with his systematic indexing by at least half a century. Concludes that though the book consists of two parts, Austin's essay alone is well worth the book price. (KK)

#183 **The moving finger, or the future of indexing** / R.D. Gee – *Indexer* (ISSN 0019-4131), 7(3)Spring 1971, p.101-113 (includes summary of discussion, p.112-113). Reprinted in: *Indexers on indexing: a selection of articles published in The Indexer* / ed. Leonard Montague Harrod for the Society of Indexers – New York, Bowker, 1978, p.368-380. (ISBN 0-8352-1099-5). See also #151.

Indexing, whether computerised or not, has yet to face its greatest problems. The improvable present is represented by indexes to individual periodicals. The Lynch programme could make some contribution here. In universal compendia like *British Technology Index* and *Engineering Index* headings become complex and in specialist fields they become cumbersome, despite excellent design philosophy. No one in his right mind will use a computer to index books, but computer assistance is necessary for abstracts and indexes. In a computer-bound world, the indexer may have something of value to offer, e.g., the computer cannot compile anything. Every book should be looked at closely to see whether an index is desired, or whether the author could structure his presentation more efficiently. If an index is necessary it should be a part of the production process – farming indexing out on a smallholding basis has not given it the consideration it deserves. With regard to the book's future, the question should be, what type of presentation is suitable for book format? (LISA 71/1162)

#184 **Computer-based indexing systems: implications for the book indexer** / John J. Eyre – *Indexer* (ISSN 0019-4131), 9(2)October 1974, p.53-57.

The terms which comprise an entry in an index can be arranged in various ways. The use of roles or facets such as 'thing-action-part-effect' under which terms can be categorized allows the use of citation orders which preserve the syntactic relationships between terms in a string. Alphabetization and rotation in context are simple methods but with certain disadvantages for the users. The citation order of the B.T.I. results in a detailed index using punctuation to indicate relationships. PRECIS incorporates prepositions which preserve the context when strings are shunted to create the necessary entries. Articulated indexes use natural language phrases displayed under selected subject headings. These methods could be used to construct book indexes. (Original abstract)

#185 **Indexing methods used by some abstracting and indexing services** / K.G.B. Bakewell – *Indexer* (ISSN 0019-4131), 10(1)April 1976, p.3-8. Reprinted in: *Indexers on indexing: a selection of articles published in The Indexer* / ed. Leonard Montague Harrod for the Society of Indexers – New York, Bowker, 1978, p.317-322. (ISBN 0-8352-1099-5). See also #151.

Various methods used for compiling the subject indexes of abstracting and indexing services are described, with particular reference to *Applied Science and Technology Index, British Technology Index* [BTI]*, Education Index, Current Journals in Education, World Textile Abstracts, Library and Information Science Abstracts*, the abstracting journals issued by Anbar Publications Ltd., and *Sociology of Education Abstracts*. The possibilities of a standardised system are considered, and the importance of a good alphabetical index is stressed if the arrangement of the service is a systematic one. (Original abstract)

Argues that BTI is certainly an alphabetical index, but has a built-in classified structure. Complex subjects are indexed as specifically as possible according to a predetermined formula developed by Ranganathan for his Colon Classification. The resulting heading can be quite formidable and the system also means that a large number of cross-references are necessary. For this reason many people find BTI difficult to use. The BTI system also provides a systematic approach to the construction of subject headings which appear to be lacking in so many other methods. (KK)

40 COMPUTERIZATION

40.10 Overview

#186 **Bibliographical indexes** / E.J. Coates – In: *Computer Typesetting Conference, London University, July 1964: Report of proceedings* – London, Institute of Printing, 1965, p.44-49.

The author has been asked to mention how the editor of a bibliographical index views the prospect of computer typesetting, and what the particular requirements of bibliographical indexes are in relation to this impending development. The non-conventional printing system used for the *British Technology Index* (BTI) was first adopted by the *British National Bibliography* in 1961. The system comprises preparation of master copy by Varityper, transfer of the copy to film by Fotolist camera, and running off by offset lithography. Discusses the inherent limitations associated with each stage of index production. Emphasizes that the publishing organization of an index is not likely to think of computerization in its typesetting application alone, and that there are two clerical tasks in index production: (1) the maintenance of an authority file and (2) the generation of cross-references from the subject-headings given. Summarizes the requirements for and operations of BTI to be computerized. (KK)

#187 **Mechanized information storage and retrieval** / R.T. Kimber – In: *British librarianship and information science, 1966-1970* / ed. H.A. Whatley – London, Library Association, 1972, p.150-167. (ISBN 0-85365-175-2).

There has been considerable activity in UK directed towards the machine generation of index entries for published bibliographies. M.F. Lynch and his co-workers at the Sheffield University have concentrated on articulated indexes of the type used in the *Chemical Abstracts*. They approached the problem by devising rules which introduced the idea of using prepositions as points of articulation. The *British Technology Index* (BTI) faced major problem of currency and a special problem in having to operate with a small staff where staff changes and absences due to illness cause significant disturbances to the flow of work. Based on a research programme which commenced in 1964, and a feasibility study undertaken, with OSTI support, by the University of Newcastle upon Tyne Computing Laboratory in 1966-67, the program suite developed for BTI performs producing two kinds of cross-references. For this purpose, punctuation between terms is used to signal the forms of manipulation to be required. By means of these manually-signalled computer manipulations, approximately 98 per cent of the requirements are met. The remaining 2 per cent of cases are handled by manual routines. The changeover to computer-aided typesetting of BTI took place in July 1969. The index entries produced for the *British National Bibliography* by D. Austin's PRECIS system represent a mid-point in the spectrum of index types, from the pure natural language phrases of Lynch to the bare strings of terms found in BTI. (KK)

#188 **Indexing and abstracting services** / P.F. Broxis – In: *British librarianship and information science, 1966-1970* / ed. H.A. Whatley – London, Library Association, 1972, p.90-102. (ISBN 0-85365-175-2). See also #297.

Computer science is now at the stage of third generation machine. Among services in this category are the British *MEDLARS*, the Chemical Society's Research Unit in *Information Retrieval Project*, and the *British Technology Index* (BTI), all of which are programmed for the ICL KDF9 computer. One spin-off of computer technology is computer-typesetting. Among typesetting machines Digiset is used in the case of BTI. Photon is used in the case of abstracting and indexing services of IEE. Another service aiming towards computer-typesetting is the *World Textile Abstracts*, the programs of which are written on the work by M.F. Lynch at the University of Sheffield. Considerable amount of attention has been given to the indexing methodology of various subject fields. A long account is given of the possible application of the BTI indexing system to the field of educational sociology. (KK)

#189 **The Library Association** / Norman Tomlinson – In: *British librarianship and information science, 1966-1970* / ed. H.A. Whatley – London, Library Association, 1972, p.644-660 (esp. p.658). (ISBN 0-85365-175-2). See also #141.

A computerization project for *British technology index* was started late in 1965 but was terminated in May 1966 because of the inability of the contractor to make progress. A fresh study was undertaken by the Newcastle University Computing Laboratory with the aid of a £4,000 grant from the Office for Scientific and Technical Information. After the inevitable trials and tribulations of technology, *British technology index* changed to computer typesetting with the July issue 1969. The purposes were to improve currency and ensure speedier production of the annual volumes. (Excerpt from original text)

#190 **Semi automatic indexing: state of the art** / H. Fangmeyer – Neuilly-sur-Seine, NATO Advisory Group for Aerospace Research and Development, February 1974, 28p. (AGARDograph, 179).

The *British Technology Index* (BTI) is reported in the section "Chain indexing." BTI has been produced from April 1968 onwards with computer assistance. Machine assistance is focused on: (1) the generation of inversion references from given subject headings; (2) the extraction of synonym and relational references from a magnetic tape store; and (3) the production of a print-out authority list. As the subject headings are semantically organized it is the indexer who indicates the relationship between index terms. This is done by instructing computer. The second process (2) mentioned above is essentially a matching operation whereby input is compared with a store. (KK)

#191 **Correspondence** / E.J. Coates – *Indexer* (ISSN 0019-4131), 9(3)April 1975, p.122. See also #203.

The Editor of the *British Technology Index* (BTI) read an article entitled, "Physics Abstracts: 100, 1,000, 1,000,000" (*The Indexer*, 9(2)1974, p.90-91). He noticed the statement that INSPEC was the first abstracting/indexing service to computerize input and print out by computer typesetting in 1969. The Editor pointed out for the record that BTI computerized input from 1968 and commenced computer typesetting with its January [sic] 1969 issue. (KK)

40.20 Announcements and news items

#192 **Computing?** – *Liaison* (no ISSN), July 1965, p.45.

The possibility of turning over to a computer certain of the operations involved in the production of B.T.I., has been considered by the Publications Committee. Such a move would help to improve the currency of the publication, thus making it more useful. An approach is being made to the Office for Scientific and Technical Information to discuss the possibility of a grant towards the initial costs of preparing a programme for a computer. (Original text)

#193 **[An offer from Newcastle]** – *Liaison* (no ISSN), December 1966, p.95.

An offer has been accepted from the Computing Laboratory of the University of Newcastle upon Tyne to conduct a feasibility study in connection with the computerization of *British Technology Index* and a grant for the project has been made by OSTI. (Original text)

#194 **British Technology Index computer study** – *Aslib Proceedings* (ISSN 0001-253X), 19(2)February 1967, p.40.

Says that OSTI has recently granted up to £4,150 to the Library Association (LA) for a feasibility study of the computerization of the *British Technology Index* (BTI). When the project is complete, the LA will consider its economic aspects and will then decide whether or not to implement the results of the study on a production basis. The project director is E.J. Coates, Editor of BTI, and the computer research will be carried out at the University of Newcastle Computing Laboratory under the direction of Professor E.S. Page. (KK)

#195 **Publications. British Technology Index** – *Annual report of the Council of the Association for the year ending 31st December, 1967: Presented at the annual meeting in London 1968* – London, Library Association, [1968], p.20.

Following the satisfactory outcome of the computerization project, financed by the Office for Scientific and Technical Information, the Council decided to change over to computer production of British Technology Index. Initially the computer will be used up to the printer's copy stage, but computer typesetting will be considered later when equipment becomes available. (Original text)

#196 **BTI and computer indexing** – *Liaison* (no ISSN), October 1967, p.79.

The work at present being done on the problem of indexing *British Technology Index* by computer processing is described in an article in a recent issue of *Nature* as being of considerable interest for the light which will be shed on the problems of classification in the field of technology. (Excerpt from original text)

#197(#196) **BTI indexing** – *Liaison* (no ISSN), November 1967, p.86. See also #209.

An item in the last issue, under the heading, "BTI and computer indexing" referred to comments on the work being done on the development of computer assistance for *British Technology Index*. Unfortunately, the article to which it referred was wrongly attributed to *Nature*. This should have been *New Scientist*, in which the article appeared on p.189 of its issue of July 27th last. The author was Mr. C.F. Cayless. (Original text)

#198 **BTI's computer processing** – *Liaison* (no ISSN), June 1968, p.39.

With the object of improving the reliability of its currency performance, the *British Technology Index* has adopted computer processing of the clerical works. But no attempt is being made to automate the indexing process. The programmes have been developed for the KDF9 computer by the University of Newcastle Computing Laboratory, under the direction of Professor E.S. Page, and with the support of OSTI. The headings for BTI are being punched to paper tape at the BTI editorial office. Tapes are sent to Newcastle where the computer generates all necessary cross-references. From this data the computer also produces updated copies of an authority file required by the indexers to maintain consistency. At present the print-out received from Newcastle is not being utilized for computer typesetting. Further development in this direction is in hand. (KK)

#199 **British Technology Index clerical operations computerised** – *Catalogue & Index* (ISSN 0008-7629), (11)July 1968, p.7.

The Library Association announces that the *British Technology Index* (BTI) has adopted computer processing of the clerical activities, using programs developed at the Newcastle University's Computing Laboratory, with the support of OSTI. Headings for BTI entries are punched on paper tape at the BTI editorial office and sent to Newcastle, where the KDF9 computer generates all necessary cross-references, either by manipulating the terms in the input headings or by matching the input terms against a magnetic tape store of relational cross-references. Computer typesetting is expected to develop in due course. No attempt is being made to computerize the indexing process itself. (KK)

#200 **British Technology Index – computerisation** / H.D. Barry – *Strain* (ISSN 0039-2103), 4(3)July 1968, p.43.

BTI has now adopted computer processing of the clerical support activities in compiling the publication. The programs have been developed for the KDF9 computer by the University of Newcastle Computing Laboratory with the support of OSTI. No attempt is made to automate the indexing process. The BTI headings are punched to paper tape at the BTI editorial office, with which a series of operations begin in Newcastle. For the time being the print-out received from Newcastle is not being utilized for computer aided type-setting. Further development in this direction is in hand. (KK)

#201 **British Technology Index** – *Special Libraries* (ISSN 0038-6723), 59(6)July-August 1968, p.466.

The Library Association's monthly subject guide to articles in British technical journals has adopted computer processing of its clerical support activities. For information: The Library Association, 7 Ridgmount St., Store St., London, WC1. (Original text)

#202 **Computer setting** – *Liaison* (no ISSN), March 1969, p.21. See also class 20.70 Use of magnetic tape.

Since last April, *British technology index* has been using computer assistance in producing and assembling cross-references for its monthly issues and, next July, a further step in the exploitation of computers for integrated index production will be taken, when it changes to computer typesetting. *BTI* will punch headings and entries to paper tape. The tape will be processed at the University of Newcastle upon Tyne Computing Laboratory to produce a print out proof containing headings, entries and all necessary cross references. After incorporation of corrections and conversions, the computer tape will drive a high speed filmsetter. As a result, it is expected that there will be gains in both production time and time available for indexing. The *BTI* computer tape will open up the possibility of easy production of rearrangements (such as an author index) or selections from the index material. (Original text)

#203 **Computer setting** – *Liaison* (no ISSN), October 1969, p.77. See also #191.

The July issue of BTI was the first to be typeset by computer. This is the outcome of nearly five years' development of plans for computerization of BTI. An application of computer aid to cover the task of producing cross-references from headings, forming and updating an authority file, sorting and cumulating has been carried out since April 1968. There was the 16-month delay in implementing computer typesetting due to the difficulty of finding a high speed filmsetter. This problem has now been solved by use of a Digest [sic] cathode ray filmsetter. The integrated production operation is shared by the editorial staff who punched the initial data to the tape, the Computing Laboratory of the University of Newcastle upon Tyne, and the Kynoch Press, Birmingham, who are responsible for converting the computer output to enable it to drive the filmsetter in association of Oriel Computer Services. (KK)

#204 **British Technology Index production computer aided** – *Catalogue & Index* (ISSN 0008-7629), (16)October 1969, p.6. See also class 20.70 Use of magnetic tape.

The current issue of BTI demonstrates the capabilities of computer typesetting. The time factor in publishing BTI is of great importance, and computerisation will enhance an already reputable time-performance. There are no plans to automate the indexing process itself. But the question of issuing BTI in a magnetic version and making excerpts and rearrangements available in visual copy form are under consideration. The production operation is shared by the BTI editorial staff who punch the initial data on to paper tape; the Computing Laboratory at Newcastle University who carry out editorial data processing on a KDF7 computer; and the Kynoch Press of Birmingham who are responsible, in association with Oriel Computer Services Ltd, for converting the computer output to drive the high speed filmsetter. (KK)

#205 **British Technology Index** – *Aslib Proceedings* (ISSN 0001-253X), 21(10)October 1969, p.383. See also class 20.70 Use of magnetic tape.

The July issue of BTI reached a further stage in the computerization. The whole text is being computer-set, which brings the advantages of greater speed and a saving of space as compared with the previous page layout. The production procedures are described. It is suggested that a full store on magnetic tape would make it possible to provide an annual author index to BTI. (KK)

#206 **Other periodical publications** – *Annual report of the Council of the Association for the year ending 31st December, 1969: Presented at the annual meeting in London 1970* – London, Library Association, [1970], p.29.

British Technology Index changed to computer typesetting with the July issue, 1969, and *British Humanities Index* adopts this method of production in January, 1970. The principal improvement in service that should result from this is much improved currency and speedier production of the annual volumes. *B.T.I.* and *B.H.I.* adopted International A4 format and brought their cover designs up-to-date. (Original text)

#207 **[BTI's clerical operations computerized]** – *Library Review* (ISSN 0024-2535), 22(4)Winter 1969, p.227.

The July 1969 issue of BTI has put on the computer an extensive range of clerical operations. From one month's issue about five days of clerical work is saved. The long-standing backlog was virtually cleared, and the time-lag between publication of the original paper and its entry in BTI is being reduced. The integrated production operation is shared by the BTI editorial staff, the Computer Laboratory of the University of Newcastle upon Tyne, who carry out editorial data processing on a KDF9 computer, and the Kynoch Press. Up to July 1969 issue BTI's record was already much better than that of any other similar index. Wonders that why there are in UK still 11 universities and 2 university engineering laboratory libraries without BTI. (KK)

40.30 Reports by the project director and the programmer

#208 **British Technology Index – a study of the application of computer processing to index production** / E.J. Coates and I. Nicholson – In: *Organisation and handling of bibliographic records by computer: Proceedings of a conference held in Newcastle upon Tyne, July 1967* / ed. Nigel S.M. Cox and Michael W. Grose – Newcastle upon Tyne, Oriel Press, 1967, p.168-178 (includes summary of discussion, p.178). (SBN 85362-000-8).

Describes a project for the computerization of the *British Technology Index* (BTI), which is still in progress, and is being undertaken at the Computer Laboratory of the University of Newcastle upon Tyne with the assistance of a grant from OSTI. Two points are made: (1) BTI is unusual in that its small size was the deciding factor in deciding to investigate the use of computer; and (2) BTI did not propose to allow 'indexing input techniques or the analysis undertaken to be in any way conditioned by the computer.' Contents of the seven-page appendixes are: (a) the inversion algorithm; (b) a sample of input data; and (c) the inversions generated from the sample data. (KK)

#209(#208)   **Progress in automated librarianship** / C.F. Cayless – *New Scientist* (ISSN 0028-6664), 35(555)July 1967, p.188-189. See also #197.

Introduces a seminar on 'The organisation and handling of bibliographic records by computer' held at the University of Newcastle upon Tyne, 17-20 July 1967. Proceedings of the seminar recorded some of the progress that is being made towards the solution of problems met. E.J. Coates, the editor of BTI, and I. Nicholson, a member of the Newcastle team, reported the investigation covering the use of a computer for sorting operations, the listing of synonyms and of mutually related headings, printout operations including computer typesetting, and term manipulations which involves the automatic generation of cross-references and is regarded as central to the whole study. For these operations it is first necessary to make explicit certain semantic relationships between terms in subject headings. (KK)

#210(#208)   **Newcastle Seminar on the organisation and handling of bibliographical records by computers** / F.D. Cole – *Library World* (ISSN 0024-2616), 69(807)September 1967, p.80 and 82 (esp. p.80).

This is a seminar report describing: (1) the opening address by the chairman; (2) an outline of major papers given; and (3) related discussions including those of the British MARC service. Says that E.J. Coates gave a paper on study of the use of a computer by a small organization, *British Technology Index*, in collaboration with the University of Newcastle Computing Laboratory. He outlined the following areas of study: (a) sorting; (b) supply of headings from a store; (c) generation of "see" inversion references by algorithm; and (d) future computer typesetting. (KK)

#211(#208)   **[Review of] Organization and handling of bibliographic records by computer** – *Program* (ISSN 0033-0337), 1(7)October 1967, p.17-21.

This volume is the proceedings of a four-day conference held at the University of Newcastle upon Tyne in July 1967. The 16 papers presented at the conference are grouped into 5 main sections according to a rough subject classification. Coates and Nicholson's paper on BTI in the last section describes the main advantages of computerization, i.e. quicker production of copy at the end of each month, when a very tight timetable has to be followed. This investigation covers the use of a computer for sorting operations, the generation of "see" inversion references, and for typesetting. So far, the main achievement of the study has been the production or a working form of an inversion algorithm which creates all the necessary cross-references from manually assigned headings. (KK)

#212(#208) **[Review of] Organization and handling of bibliographic records by computer** / Herbert Coblans – *Unesco Bulletin for Libraries* (ISSN 0041-5243), 22(4)July-August 1968, p.196-198.

There are 16 papers and the related discussions which are arranged in 5 groups in the proceedings. Following reviews of several papers, special mention is made of Coates and Nicholson's paper on the *British Technology Index* for the reason that the most suitable field for computer application is in the production of printed indexes, where bibliographical entries are tagged at input in order to provide subject indexes (as well as authors and other ordering) and the frequent cumulations. Emphasizes that what is especially interesting in this case is the computer generation of inversion cross-references to complex subject headings, which has not been attempted before. Concludes that the seminar and the record of its proceedings are a landmark in British librarianship. (KK)

#213(#208) **Problems and some answers in bibliographic control [Review of] Organization and handling of bibliographic records by computer** / Theodore C. Hines – *Computers and the Humanities* (ISSN 0010-4817), 5(4)March 1971, p.243.

This is the record of a seminar jointly sponsored by the Library and the Computing Laboratory of the University of Newcastle upon Tyne. It is far more worthy of careful perusal than the proceedings of most similar seminars held in the United States. There are 16 papers with summaries of the discussion of each. The papers are grouped into five sections. The final paper in the last section is about efforts of automation for BTI. The desirable attributes for a system for producing a periodical index are well described, but specific information is limited to computer manipulation of the unique form of indexing terms used by BTI. Points out that this is of value in stimulating thought on less over-theorized, more customary, and more useful index entry forms. (KK)

#214 **A project to study the feasibility of the production of the British Technology Index by computer. Final report May 1968** / I. Nicholson – Newcastle upon Tyne, University of Newcastle upon Tyne Computing Laboratory, 1968, 22p. (OSTI report, 5029).

The application to OSTI for financial support to the project was forwarded in April 1966 and granted. Work started in October 1966 for an initial period of one year with the understanding that an extension would be considered if more time was found necessary. The typographical requirements of the study were still being studied in September 1967 and were completed in a further three months. The program was completed for the first time production run which took place on 19th April 1968 producing results which were very acceptable to BTI. Appended are: (1) the inversion algorithm; (2) the BTI data format; (3) programs produced for the project; (4) flow diagram of the BTI production system; and (5) examples of output obtained. (KK)

#215(#214) Report on 1st six months' production operational use of computer assembly of cross reference data and compilation of authority file / E.J. Coates, [1968], 3p. – Supplement attached to: *A project to study the feasibility of the production of the British Technology Index by computer. Final report May 1968* / I. Nicholson – Newcastle upon Tyne, University of Newcastle upon Tyne Computing Laboratory, 1968, 22p. (OSTI report, 5029).

Discusses some unsolved problems recognized by the editor of BTI after the transition to computerized data processing which started in April 1968. Concludes that a major unsolved question concerns ease of removing matter from the authority file and matching store. Required are: (1) a means of inputting deletions in random order; (2) the facility to delete a heading and its dependent inversion references by input of the heading only; and (3) to be able to input to the authority file the residue of references produced manually. (KK)

#216 The computerisation of the British Technology Index / E.J. Coates – In: *Computer based information retrieval systems* / ed. Bernard Houghton – London, Clive Bingley, 1968, p.45-63 (includes discussion, p.61-63). (SBN 85157-059-3).

At the beginning of this paper the author emphasizes that though the seminar is devoted to computer *based* information retrieval systems, the particular system which he is about to describe would be better called computer *aided*, because the production of the *British Technology Index* is *human* based. (KK)

The *British Technology Index* (BTI) is published monthly and cumulated annually. About 390 British journals are reviewed, and articles are selected for indexing. Descriptive entries are then prepared for the selected articles. Indexers then assign alphabetical subject headings, consisting of a string of terms which represents a telegraphic rendering of the contents of the article. The vocabulary used is controlled, and an authority file of all decisions is kept. At this point, the use of computers is introduced to assemble synonym and relational cross references, as well as the inversion of cross references, which lead the user to the headings chosen by the indexer. This stage of computerization has been operational since April, 1968. Detailed explanations with examples are provided on the pre-coordinated subject heading and cross reference structure of the index, as well as the manual and computer operations involved. At the completion of this first stage, a printout will be made of the authority file of headings and all types of cross references. The second stage of computerization will take the magnetic tape containing the subject heading string and cross references, apply to it a computer typesetting program, and do the printing on a film master. However, the computer typesetting equipment now available is too slow for the desired performance. At present, conventional typesetting and printing procedures are used. The principal advantage of the present stage of computerization is the gain of 2.5 days per month in indexing time. (ISA 70-897)

#217(#216) [Review of] Computer based information retrieval systems / Frederick

G. Kilgour – *Journal of Library Automation* (ISSN 0022-2240), 2(3) September 1969, p.178-179.

The book contains six papers that were presented at a special course in April 1968 at the Liverpool School of Librarianship. The objective of the course was to survey the major computer based information retrieval systems operating in the United Kingdom. Five papers describe systems all depict retrieval from files of journal articles. The five systems are: MEDLARS, the Science Citation Index (SCI), the Chemical Tiles (CT) and the Chemical-Biological Activities (CBAC), the Institution of Electrical Engineers (IEE), and the British Technology Index (BTI) which the reviewer regards a minor computer application to production. The final paper is G.A. Somerfield's the state of the art analysis of computer based IR systems. (KK).

#218(#216) **[Review of] Computer based information retrieval systems** / Epsevia Vassilion – *American Documentation* (ISSN 0096-946X), 20(4) October 1969, p.388.

This is a compilation of six papers presented at the Liverpool School of Librarianship in 1968. They represent the UK major undertakings and studies in the computer and information retrieval field. Of the six papers half are devoted to efficiency study of existing American systems, such as MEDLARS, SCI and CAS. The book serves as an excellent introduction to information retrieval system for students. Each paper presents a particular British application or study of systems dealt with. Says that E.J. Coates deals with the technical aspects of the British Technology Index (BTI), but that for the reader unfamiliar with BTI, the paper demands considerably more concentration than do the others. One of its peculiarities is that Coates points out that it is not computer-based but computer-assisted. (KK)

#219(#216) **[Review of] Computer based information retrieval systems** [Review in French] / Eric de Grolier – *Bulletin des Bibliotheques de France* (ISSN 0006-2006), 16(12) Decembre 1971, p.1035.

This book is a compilation of six papers presented at a course on the automatic (or rather, semi-automatic) retrieval systems held at the Liverpool School of Librarianship in April 1968. It deals with MEDLARS, search strategies based on the Science Citation Index, production of the British Technology Index using a computer, and two experiences in SDI at the University of Nottingham and the Institution of Electrical Engineers. The book ends with "the state of the arts" by G.A. Somerfield of the OSTI. (KK)

#220 **Computerisation of British Technology Index: man-machine collaboration in the production of indexes** / E.J. Coates – *INSPEL* (ISSN 0019-0217), 3(3-4) July-October 1968, p.147-163.

Paper read at the 34th Session of the General Council of IFLA, held in Frankfurt am Main, 18-24 August 1968. BTI's subject heading is a highly abbreviated summary of the subject content. A given subject heading produces a given set of cross references. Some of the cross references are produced by manipulating the elements in the subject heading string; others are derived from extraneous sources, i.e. lists of synonyms and hierarchically related lists of terms. A byproduct is a printout authority file of indexing decisions, which indexers find it essential to consult in order to maintain consistency. These operations have been for the last 6 years carried out manually by indexers and clerical staff. 15 to 20% of indexers' time has been spent in these ancillary activities. It is the clerical operations that should be computerized. The work of refinement and elaboration of the manual procedures to be embodied in a computer program occupied 6 weeks in the summer of 1964. The BTI system was submitted to the Computing Laboratory of the University of Newcastle upon Tyne during the summer of 1966. Programming for data processing was completed and tested about 12 months. The results of trials were incorporated in 3 of the monthly issue in the summer of 1967. The LA decided to adopt computerization, which came into effect with the April 1968 issue. Computerized operations are illustrated with examples. (KK)

#221(#220) **[IFLA meeting in Frankfurt]** – *Liaison* (no ISSN), June 1968, p.41.

The LA has agreed to take part in a joint session of two sections of IFLA which will discuss the problems of bibliographic work of special libraries. It is suggesting that Mr. E.J. Coates might submit a paper to the joint session on the computerization of BTI processes, and, if this is accepted, Mr. Coates will be included in the LA delegation to this year's IFLA meeting in Frankfurt. (Original text)

#222(#220) **Minutes of meeting of Special Libraries Section of IFLA, Wednesday, August 21, 1968, Frankfurt/Main** – *INSPEL* (ISSN 0019-0217), 3(3-4)July-October 1968, p.103-104.

In the section 5, under the heading 'Papers presented', it was reported that a number of papers had been handed in for presentation in this session, i.e.: Mr. Marc Chauveinc, Grenoble; Mr. Eric J. Coates, London; Mr. F. Wilfred Lancaster, Washington; and Mr. Arthur Gropp, Washington. Of the four only Mr. Coates was present. He summarized his elaborate paper on the computerization of the British Technology Index. (KK)

#223(#220) **Gutenberg, Frankfurters and IFLA** / Karl A. Baer – *Special Libraries* (ISSN 0038-6723), 59(10)December 1968, p.797-799 (esp. p.798).

This is a report of the 34th Session of the General Council of IFLA (August 18-24, 1968) held in Frankfurt am Main. A series of papers on the organization and support of special libraries, with particular stress on their bibliographic activities, had been initiated at the 1966 IFLA meeting in The Hague. Says that this was continued with E.J. Coates' (British Technology Index, London) excellent presentation of "The computerisation of the British Technology Index." Coates fielded questions more successfully than the reporter could, following his reading (in the author's absence) of a paper on MEDLARS by F.W. Lancaster,

NLM, Washington, D.C. (KK)

#224 Computer assistance in the production of BTI / E.J. Coates – *Library Association Record* (ISSN 0024-2195), 70(10)October 1968, p.255-257.

The first stage of the *BTI* computerization project is now in operation and the transition from manual processing has passed smoothly. The computer generates inversion "see" references from input subject headings, extracts relevant relational and synonym cross references from a magnetic tape store, and produces a monthly up-dated authority file. The object of the change is to provide more time per month for indexing than has been available when these processes were performed manually by indexers. The ultimate result will be that the currency performance of *BTI* will be less sensitive to minor staff emergencies than hitherto. An account is given of the development of the project, and the future possibilities to which it may give rise are briefly surveyed. (Original abstract)

#225 Computerised data processing for British Technology Index / E.J. Coates – *Indexer* (ISSN 0019-4131), 6(3)Spring 1969, p.97-101. Reprinted in: *Indexers on indexing: a selection of articles published in The Indexer* / ed. Leonard Montague Harrod for the Society of Indexers – New York, Bowker, 1978, p.404-408. (ISBN 0-8352-1099-5). See also #151.

The computer produces cross-reference copy from a given set of subject headings. This is achieved partly by extracting references from a magnetic tape store and partly by manipulating the component words in a subject heading according to prescriptions in the program. Examples of these processes are given. The complete process takes a little over an hour each month leading to a considerable rise in the productivity of the indexing staff. A by-product is a monthly updated authority file of indexing decisions produced as computer print-out. Plans for computer typesetting are well advanced. (LISA 69/973)

#226(#225) History of indexing societies: Part III, Society of Indexers / Hazel K. Bell – *Indexer* (ISSN 0019-4131), 21(1)April 1998, p.33-36.

This part of the History returns to the Society of Indexers in the UK and traces a further ten years of development. Describes that the inexorable coming of the computer continued. The index to the volume 6 of *The Indexer*, 1968-69, shows articles titled: Computers and indexes; Computer indexing of archives; Computerised data processing for *British Technology Index*; and Computerized data banks in science and technology. (KK)

#227(#225) The Indexer thirty-odd years ago / Hazel K. Bell – *Indexer* (ISSN 0019-4131), 21(4)October 1999, p.186-189 (esp. p.187).

Volume 16 [sic] of *The Indexer* ran through 1968-9, with a total of 192 pages. ... Articles on computers are beginning to proliferate in *The Indexer*. In this issue [no.3], E.J. Coates writes (five pages) on 'computerised data processing for *British Technology Index'* which 'attempts to record articles from British technical journals within seven weeks of their original publication.' Each month's issue of the index comprised 2000 to 2500 entries, plus 5000 to 6000 cross-references generated by the subject index headings attached to entries; this task, of producing cross-references, was assigned to the computer. Coates reports: 'The adoption of the computer assistance led to a considerable rise in the productivity of the indexing staff. After four months computer-assisted operation, the former backlog of work had been eliminated.' (Excerpt from original text)

40.40 Hardware and software

#228 **British Technology Index computerisation** – *Program* (ISSN 0033-0337), 2(2)July 1968, p.70.

With the object of improving the reliability of its currency performance, BTI has adopted computer processing of the clerical support activities needed in compiling the publication. The programs have been developed for the KDF9 computer by the University of Newcastle Computing Laboratory with the support of OSTI. No attempt is made to automate the indexing process. The BTI headings are punched to paper tape at the BTI editorial office, which is followed by a series of operations in Newcastle. For the time being the print-out received from Newcastle is not being utilized for computer-aided typesetting. Further development in this direction is in hand. (KK)

#229 **British Technology Index** / D.J. Foskett and M.J. Humby – In their: **Documentation of education in the United Kingdom with an account of other semi-mechanised and mechanised systems of interest** – In: *EUDISED: European Documentation and Information System for Education. Volume II, National reports* – Strasbourg, Council of Europe, Documentation Centre for Education in Europe, 1969, p.78-97 (esp. p.90). (ERIC report, ED 040 716).

Describes that the first application of computer assistance to the production of BTI came with the use of programs prepared by the University of Newcastle upon Tyne Computing Laboratory to generate inversion cross references from input headings, to extract from store synonym and relational cross references, to sort, and to produce a printout authority file. All programs were for the English Electric KFD 9 computer. The next stage will make use of computer typesetting techniques for the production of BTI itself. This stage may come into operation in 1969 if the Linotron 505 setter is found to be suitable. Success in applying these computer programs to BTI is of interest in connection with the mechanisation of the *British Education Index*. (KK)

#230 **Other periodical publications** – *Annual report of the Council of the Association for the year ending 31st December, 1970: Presented at the annual meeting in London 1971* – London, Library Association, [1971], p.28.

British Humanities Index adopted computer typesetting in January 1970, while *British Technology Index* moves on to a third generation computer in 1972. Circulation of *British Humanities Index* has risen by some 20 per cent, while both *British Technology Index* and *Journal of Librarianship* have slightly improved on last year's figures. (Original text)

#231 **Other periodical publications** – *Annual report of the Council of the Association for the year ending 31st December, 1971: Presented at the annual meeting in London 1972* – London, Library Association, [1972], p.26.

British Technology Index moves to a third generation computer in January, 1972. Circulation of *British Technology Index*, *British Humanities Index* and *Journal of Librarianship* remained constant. (Original text)

#232 **Generating and printing indexes by computer** / Lucille H. Campey – London, Aslib, 1972, 101p. (Aslib occasional publication, 11) (SBN 85142-047-8).

The aims of the report are: (1) to locate information about computer techniques for generating and printing indexes; (2) to establish details about operational systems (i.e. computer configuration, costs and use option); and (3) to determine the availability of programs. Major findings include: (a) systems identified cover a wide range of index types; (b) details have been ascertained for 118 systems; (c) 20 of the total number represent IBM software; (d) there are far more studies of the KWIC index and its variants; (e) automated compilation of printed indexes usually involves some human intervention; and (f) many systems provide additional facilities. There is a detailed list of descriptions of computer systems available for printing indexes. Techniques for generating index entries by computer are considered in the context of four main categories: (i) KWIC indexes; (ii) KWIC variants; (iii) articulated subject indexes; and (iv) rotated indexing systems (other than KWIC). The *British Technology Index* (BTI) is treated in the category (iv). The BTI system was originally designed for the English Electric KDF9 computer and is currently being rewritten for an ICL 4/70 computer. Program language will be COBOL and ASSEMBLE. New system is made available when complete. (KK)

#233 **A survey of index generation programs** / Lucille H. Campey – *Information Storage and Retrieval* (ISSN 0020-0271), 9(8) August 1973, p.441-448.

A total of 118 computer systems have been located, 55 of which are UK systems and 20 are IBM software packages. Index types covered in the survey were: (1) machine formatted indexes – subject index listings, coordinate indexes, book catalogues and bibliographies, citation indexes; (2) machine generated index entries – KWIC indexes, KWIC variants, articulated subject indexes, rotational indexing systems (other than KWIC), concordances, book indexes, SLIC (Selective Listing in Combination) and TABLEDEX. Bases for comparison were lead term or entry point, context for the lead term, author and bibliographic details and link key. The *British Technology Index* (BTI) is treated in the category of rotational indexing systems (other than KWIC). Another system treated in the same category is PRECIS. These two systems are developed in the UK, and either software is other than that of IBM. (KK)

50 USER-ORIENTED EDUCATION AND TRAINING

50.10 Discussion meetings, lectures and workshops on BTI indexing system

#234 **Midlands Branch** – *Aslib Proceedings* (ISSN 0001-253X), 14(8)August 1962, p.217.

Announces that the Branch has arranged four meetings for the coming months. All these meetings will be held at 6.30 p.m. at the Birmingham Engineering and Building Centre. Meetings and speakers are: (1) Monday 1st October, Mr. D. Bullivant on 'The SfB system of filing and the standardization of documents'; (2) Tuesday 4th December, Mr. J.R. Davies on 'Punched cards in library routine'; (3) Wednesday 6th February 1963, Mr. E.J. Coates on 'The British Technology Index'; and (4) the Annual General Meeting will be held on Monday 25th March 1963, when Mr. R. Sheldon of the National Institute for Research in Nuclear Science, Harwell, will deliver a paper on information retrieval. (KK)

#235 **Discussion meetings 1962/1963** / E. Alan Baker – *Indexer* (ISSN 0019-4131), 3(2)Autumn 1962, p.82.

The Society of Indexers will hold six meetings between on Tuesday, October 16, 1962 and on Thursday, April 25, 1963. All meetings will be held at the Library Association, Chaucer House, Malet Place, London W.C.1, at 6.0 p.m. preceded by tea at 5.30. A meeting with E.J. Coates, FLA, Editor, on "British Technology Index" is scheduled to be held on Thursday, February 28, 1963. (KK)

#236 **Training in indexing** – *Aslib Proceedings* (ISSN 0001-253X), 16(11)November 1964, p.329. See also #149 and #150.

The Society of Indexers is to run a course of ten weekly lectures on indexing at the School of Librarianship, North-Western Polytechnic, beginning on Wednesday 20th January 1965. Mr. E.J. Coates, Editor of BTI, will give a paper of 'Scientific and technical indexes.' The lectures will be from 6.30 to 8.00 p.m.; refreshments can be obtained at the Polytechnic refectory. The fee is 30s for the whole course or 5s for each lecture. Applications to attend should be made to Mr. G. Norman Knight, 3 Western Mansions, Barnet, Hertfordshire, as soon as possible and in any event not later than 1st January 1965. (KK)

#237 **One-day workshop on BTI** – *Library Association Record* (ISSN 0024-2195), 71(10) October 1969, p.310. See also #238.

A one-day workshop on the *British Technology Index* (BTI), promoted by the Liverpool

School of Librarianship and Information Work and the BTI for the benefit of technologists, industrial information officers, and librarians working in industry or in the reference departments of public libraries, will be held on 11 November. The course is user oriented. The principles and policy underlying the preparation of the BTI will be outlined as a preliminary to detailed treatment of its day-to-day use in retrieving and monitoring information on current and retrospective topics. The fee will be £3 and applications should be made to the school. (KK)

#238 **British Technology Index Workshop at Liverpool** – *Catalogue & Index* (ISSN 0008-7629), (16)October 1969, p.6. See also #237.

A Workshop on the British Technology Index is to be held at the Liverpool School of Librarianship on November 11. Speakers will include Mr E.J. Coates, (Editor of BTI), J. Sharp (ICI Fibres) and G. Rowland, (LADSIRLAC). Full details from Mr Bernard Houghton, Dept. of Librarianship, College of Commerce, Tithebarn Street, Liverpool. (Original text)

#239 **SIMULE: an experiment in teaching information storage and retrieval** / C. David Batty and Candy Schwartz – *Journal of Education for Librarianship* (ISSN 0022-0604), 17(4)Spring 1977, p.238-246.

The Graduate School of Library Science at McGill University has been developing courses in the area of information storage and retrieval. A laboratory where students could gain experiential training was essential to the theoretical understanding and practical work. The laboratory of information retrieval systems and the Self Instructional Modules Using Laboratory Experience (SIMULEs) that accompany it were established. The major components of the laboratory are the 12 or so different indexes. There are 7 groups of SIMULEs, 5 of which concerning different families of indexes. SIMULEs 21 and 22 discuss pre-coordinate alphabetical subject headings of conventional type, such as the Library of Congress and Sear's and the alphabetico-specific headings created by the application of predetermined formulae. The component terms of the subject headings are combined according to the following formula: Output, Process, Agent, Material, Type of library, Place, Time. This combination order is derived from the model developed by Coates and used by him for the *British Technology Index*. (KK)

#240 **Course on computer-produced indexes, 12 and 13 October 1977 at Aslib Headquarters** – *Aslib Information* (ISSN 0305-0033), 5(7)July 1977, p.[23-24].

The announcement says that the course consists of 7 sessions, 4 of which are given in the first day and 3 in the second day. Session 1, Open discussion, will ask students to give five-minute talks concerning their systems; Session 2, General introduction, including basic components of a printed indexes and vocabulary control; Session 3, *KWIC, KWOC, SLIC* and their variants; Session 4, String input systems – *PRECIS, Articulated Subject Index* and

British Technology Index; Session 5, Points of comparison between different index formats, including evaluation procedures; Session 6, Different physical forms of output; and Session 7, Using a bureau versus do it yourself, available packages and use of computers. (KK)

#241 Course on computer-produced indexes, 15 and 16 January 1979 at Aslib Headquarters – *Aslib Information* (ISSN 0305-0033), 6(10-11) October-November 1978, p.[35-36].
For abstract, see #240. (KK)

#242 Course on computer-produced indexes, 4 and 5 June 1979 at Aslib Headquarters – *Aslib Information* (ISSN 0305-0033), 7(4) April 1979, p.91.
For abstract, see #240. (KK)

#243 Course on computer-produced indexes, 22 and 23 June 1981 at Aslib Headquarters – *Aslib Information* (ISSN 0305-0033), 9(6)June 1981, p.169.
For abstract, see #240. (KK)

50.20 Instruction in use of bibliographic tools including BTI

#244 Technical college libraries: 2 Tuition in library use / J. Cowley – *Technical Education and Industrial Training* (ISSN 0374-4701), 6(9)September 1964, p.442-444.
Most of the 1,800 students attending Mid-Herts College fall into the 16-21 age group. The full-time students attend commercial, science, engineering, or arts courses leading to GCE 'O'- and 'A'-levels, RSA, and ONC qualifications. The block-release and day-release students attend craft, technician, laboratory and ONC courses. Beyond this range, the student is transferred to the College of Technology, for which the Further Education establishments act 'feeder' colleges. (Original abstract)
After preliminary training course, the student is encouraged to trace up-to-date information using the Applied Science and Technology Index and the British Technology Index, various abstracting services, bibliographies and book lists. (KK)

#245 Tuition in library use as part of Open University preparatory courses / B.L. Pearce – *Library Review* (ISSN 0024-2535), 25(7)Autumn 1976, p.254-256.
Emphasizes the need for library instruction as a means of providing users with a full appreciation of the informational value of libraries. In the case of Open University students it might be logical for such instruction to be given during the preparatory course. Outlines an example library instruction programme comprising 12 evening lectures with stress on practical work and the use of basic bibliographical tools. At the example library students on the science or technology courses would be introduced to the following items: (1) classified catalogue and indexes to other media; (2) encyclopedias and reference works;

(3) bibliographies such as BNB and CBI; (4) periodical indexes such as BTI and ASTI, and abstracts such as Engineering Index and Science Abstracts; and (5) generalia. Students are requested to seek information on the given topics by using the above-mentioned tools, together with the library staff in the first part of the tuition. (KK)

#246 **The design and development of a course of information retrieval for engineering students** / Nancy Fjallbrant – *European Journal of Engineering Education* (ISSN 0304-3797), 2(3)1977, p.213-222.

Chalmers University of Technology, Gothenburg, Sweden, has about 4,000 undergraduates and some 600 postgraduates. The undergraduate programme takes 4 to 5 years. It was decided to design and develop a course in library instruction that was directly related to the needs of engineering students in their general course. A basic plan for a 14 hour course in information retrieval (IR) was drawn up. The plan consists of: (1) 1 hour lecture, Introduction to scientific communication; (2) 1 hour lecture, Methods of information searching; (3) 2 x 5 hour "laboratory" sessions, at about 1 week's interval: (a) Conventional tools for IR such as *Engineering Index*, *British Technology Index*, *Artikkel Indeks*, plus subject-related tools; (b) the use of *Science Citation Index* and similar tools such as the *Index to Scientific Reviews*. Starting point for laboratory session for above (b) is the reference list obtained during session (a); and (4) 2 hour "home study" for the presentation of a list of references. The 14 hour course in IR is attended by some 600 engineering undergraduates per year. After graduation they go to practical work directly and good comments have come from industry. (KK)

#247 **A guide to searching the engineering literature** / Nestor Osorio – Boca Raton, FL, J. Hurley Associates, 1979. (Educational programs in science).

This audio-visual program, which deals with 7 secondary information tools, consists of two parts. Part I: Non-US Government publications; (1) *Applied Science and Technology Index*, (2) *Engineering Index*, (3) *Physics Abstracts*, and (4) *British Technology Index*. Part II: US Government publications; (5) *Government Reports Announcements and Index*, (6) *Scientific and Technical Aerospace Reports*, and (7) *Energy Research Abstracts*. Each of the 7 works is examined for format, scope of technical interest, content and accessing procedure. Discussion of each work is based upon a scientific search topic. Program materials consist of a set of 96 visuals in 35 mm slide format, 2 audio cassettes and text. The audiotapes are about 75 minutes in total length. Program materials are equally suited for group presentation and audio-tutorial study. (KK)

60 USER STUDY AND LABORATORY EVALUATION

For subscribers' opinion on BTI, see #127 and #265.

60.10 Editor's opinion on index evaluation

#248 **Card indexes or printed pages – physical substrates in index evaluation** / E.J. Coates – *Indexer* (ISSN 0019-4131), 10(2)October 1976, p.60-68. Reprinted in: *Indexers on indexing: a selection of articles published in The Indexer* / ed. Leonard Montague Harrod for the Society of Indexers – New York, Bowker, 1978, p.128-136. (ISBN 0-8352-1099-5). See also #151.

Based on a talk given at the Study Institute on Printed Subject Indexes, Aberystwyth, July 1975. General ideas on indexing have been greatly influenced by performance testing, which began in the 1960s. It is suggested that the exclusive use in these tests of the single-record-per-index-card form could limit the generality of the ideas to be derived from the tests. Panoramic display forms of index (of which the printed page is the commonest example) offer users enhanced mobility in relation to the file, which in turn facilitates recognition of elements of structure in the displayed sequence. Structured data may be preferentially accessible to enquiry or comprehension. Typographical resources supply structure to printed indexes, in particular by forming visual blocks of conceptually homogeneous material – to the extent that the mechanics of filing order and the grammar of the indexing language allows or facilitates this. Examples from the *British National Bibliography* (PRECIS) and the *British Technology Index* are given for illustration, the problems of the classified printed index are mentioned briefly, and suggestions are made on the lines of research on printed indexes which might usefully be pursued. (Original abstract)

60.20 INSPEC

INSPEC was an outgrowth of the Science Abstracts service and registered trademark of the Institution of Electrical Engineers (IEE), London, UK.

#249 **Laboratory evaluation of printed subject indexes, Part 1: Design and methodology** / T.M. Aitchison, Katherine H. Lavelle and Angela M. Hall – London, Institution of Electrical Engineers, March 1970, 13p. (INSPEC report, R.70/5) (ISBN 0-85296-403-X).

A methodology is described which has been established for the evaluation of the performance of printed subject indexes. The design of a laboratory evaluation which will use this methodology is detailed. The indexes to be tested are: INSPEC (*Science Abstracts*), *Engineering Index*, *Applied Science and Technology Index*, and *British*

Technology Index. (Original abstract)

#250 **Laboratory evaluation of printed [subject] indexes, Part II: Results and discussion of methodology** / T.M. Aitchison and Angela M. Hall – London, Institution of Electrical Engineers, February 1973, 64p. (INSPEC report, R.73/17) (ISBN 0-85296-414-5).

A 'laboratory' evaluation of the performance of printed indexes is reported in which a set of questions were used to search four indexes: *Science Abstracts*, *Engineering Index*, *Applied Science and Technology Index*, and *British Technology Index*. Because of deficiencies in the methodology only minor results were obtained. These methodological difficulties and the associated practical problems are discussed. (Original abstract)

#251 **User preference in printed indexes** / Angela M. Hall – London, Institution of Electrical Engineers, July 1972, 86p. (INSPEC report, R.72/7) (OSTI report, 5131) (ISBN 0-85296-406-4). See also #253.

A study of users' preferences for particular printed indexes and the assessment of the characteristics of these indexes are reported. The design of a suitable questionnaire for, and the choice of representative sample of, 2 user groups are discussed. 2 user groups are: (1) library and information staff and (2) scientific and technical staff. They were selected from the subscribers to *Science Abstracts* (SA) in the UK. The abstracts journals and indexes most frequently subscribed to are those which have a wide subject coverage. It is the suitability of coverage and the cost which are the critical factors in the choice of abstracts journals and indexes. The top-three are SA (135/143), BTI (91/143) and EI (88/143). The most frequently used publications are EI (73%), SA (72%) and BTI (63%). BTI (38%) is referred to most frequently as a first choice and EI (13%). EI (36%) is more frequently used as a second choice for a more extensive search. Suitability of subjects coverage, currency and accuracy are considered to be the most important features of an abstract journal or index. There is no single characteristic which makes an index particularly easy to use, but suitable subject headings, cross-references and additional indexes are all important. (KK)

#252 (#251) **Methodology and results of some user studies on secondary information services** / Angela M. Hall – In: *EURIM: a European Conference on Research into the Management of Information Services and Libraries, 20-22 November 1973, UNESCO, Place de Fontenoy, Paris 7e, France* – London, Aslib, 1974, p.31-37 (includes discussion, p.37). (ISBN 0-85142-059-1). See also #265.

User studies carried out at INSPEC are discussed under the headings: (1) information gathering activities of scientists and engineers; (2) user preference in printed indexes including the subjective approach, quick reference versus exhaustive searches, subject index headings, cross references; (3) *Science Abstracts* covering use of cross references, index entries. Results indicate information officers and scientists employ differing search techniques; many users scan all references under subject headings in preference to using the alphabetical arrangement; users have greater confidence in an index with obligatory cross-references; there is no correlation between the use of cross-references and ease of use of the indexes. Tables detail results of the studies. (LISA 75/618)

In the second study (2) above, describes that the index characteristics which were thought to be more important were those which assisted quicker and easier index use. BTI is assessed by being compared with the Engineering Index (EI). BTI is used as a first choice by 38% of its subscribers, which is the highest score, while a figure of 13% is noted for EI. For the publications used most frequently as a second choice the situation is reversed showing 17% and 36%. As to the subject headings of BTI, 60% of its users thought them suitable and 4% found them unsuitable. A preference is expressed for the cross-references of BTI, 71% of users found them acceptable and only 2% indicate to the contrary. 29% of BTI users have confidence in retrieving the relevant items, 19% of EI users have such confidence. Similarly, 28% of EI users lack confidence, and 20% for BTI users. Participants are surprised at the rating given to BTI that does not provide abstract. (KK)

#253 **User preference in published indexes** / Angela M. Gould [nee Hall] – *Journal of the American Society for Information Science* (ISSN 0002-8231), 25(5)September-October 1974, p.279-286. See also #251.

A survey of users' opinions of various printed subject indexes to abstract journals, particularly *Science Abstracts*, was carried out at INSPEC by means of a questionnaire sent to subscribers to *SA*, i.e., library staff and scientists. Results are discussed and illustrated: (1) indexes most frequently used and subscribed were *Science Abstracts*, *British Technology Index*, *Engineering Index*; (2) important characteristics include suitable coverage, accuracy, currency, ease of use, layout, suitable and precise subject index headings, and cross references – reasons for preferences are illustrated as applied to each abstract journal, and use explained; (3) differences of use between library staff and scientists include the information officer's problem of limited subject knowledge, but they use more 'see-references' and supplementary search tools. Recent changes in the index to *Science Abstracts* take account of the users' preferences. (LISA 74/3754)

#254(#251, #253) **The essentials or desiderata of the bibliographic record as discovered by research** / D. Kathryn Weintraub – *Library Resources & Technical Services* (ISSN 0024-2527), 23(4)Fall 1979, p.391-405.

Research indicates that use of the existing bibliographical apparatus is often successful: users find what they are looking for. This research has been concentrated on the use of sources where access is defined through choice of entry and where the user wanted to find a given item/author/subject. Suggestions for improving choice of entry include increasing the number of access points or analysing the problems involved in choice of entry to enable a consistent set of principles to be formed. The same suggestions have been made regarding subject entry. Research findings require synthesis into a coherent system. (LISA

80/3174)

Regarding subject entry Angela M. Gould's study of user preferences in subject indexes are referred to, i.e. only 13% of the subscribers used *Engineering Index* (EI) first as compared with 38% who used *British Technology Index* (BTI) first. This is said to be due to BTI's coextensive subject heading. But the author argues that the tables in this study also show that users' first choice of BTI is due to its currency. (KK)

60.30 EPSILON

EPSILON stands for the 'Evaluation of Printed Subject Indexes by Laboratory investigatiON' project carried out at the College of Librarianship Wales, Aberystwyth, UK.

See also #161.

#255 On the generation and searching of entries in printed subject indexes / E. Michael Keen – *Journal of Documentation* (ISSN 0022-0418), 33(1) March 1977, p.15-45.

A classification of entry types is offered, based on index term context, predominant term order, and between-term function words. Then a multiple entry generation scheme is described, comprising rules for term manipulation, input and output. After discussing access points and cross reference measures, a preliminary linguistic analysis is given, showing links with psycholinguistics. BTI is classified in 'Chain procedure subject headings' which is one of the seven index entry types in EPSILON. BTI is characterized by Role operators (as input term order), Progressive truncation (as term manipulation algorithm of chain procedure) and Citation order (as a derivative). Chain procedure as implemented in BTI brings indirect entries such as 'see references,' which has always been assumed to gain index space for an increase in search steps and page turning. But the way that blocks or pockets of entries are presented to the searcher is vital, and a preliminary look at some of the needs for typographical distinctions in subject entries has been made by Coates and on EPSILON. (KK)

#256 On the performance of nine printed subject index entry types: a selective report of EPSILON / E. Michael Keen – Aberystwyth, College of Librarianship Wales, Department of Information Systems Studies, September 1978, 77p. (BLRDD report, 5475) (ISBN 0-904020-11-8).

Reports the main results of an evaluation of printed subject indexes by laboratory investigation known as EPSILON. The aim was to test the effects of index entry variations from the user's viewpoint. Comparisons were made of 3 design variables: (1) index term context; (2) function words; and (3) term order. 7 test indexes were constructed: LEAD Term (without context), Rotated String (as KWOC or KWIC), Articulated Prepositional (after M.F. Lynch), Shunted Relational (as PRECIS, after D.W. Austin) and Chain Procedure (as BTI, after E.J. Coates). 9 entry types were constructed. The test collection and search requests were in library and information science. Details are given of the indexing methods; characterisation of the indexes and searches; whole indexes search tests; part-indexes scanning tests; and performance results of recall, precision, time, effort, relevance prediction and performances. Comparisons showed that index term context provides benefit in screening out irrelevant material, thus improving precision. Levels of function words showed only a minute performance advantage for full provision. Term order was tested as sentence-like active form and the fragmented form of articulated and shunted. No significant performance differences emerged. Chain Procedure led to weakness in recall, time and search effort. (Original abstract amended by KK)

The report was, in length, a 15% selection of the full report published in microfiche form: *Evaluation of printed subject indexes by laboratory investigations: final report for the period October 1973-March 1978* / E. Michael Keen and Alan Wheatley – Aberystwyth, College of Librarianship Wales, Department of Information Systems Studies, June 1978, 466p. (BLRDD report, 5454). (KK)

#257(#256)   **[Review of] On the performance of nine printed subject index entry types** / David Batty – *Library Quarterly* (ISSN 0024-2519), 50(1)January 1980, p.150-151.

Mentions that the selective EPSILON report is slender (only 77 pages, 21 of which are appendices), but that it contains a wealth of information. EPSILON represents five years of study of the characteristics and performance of types of printed subject index mainly in terms of (1) index term context; (2) function words; and (3) term order. The types range from familiar rotated string indexes (like KWOC), through shunted relational (like PRECIS), to chain procedure (like British Technology Index). EPSILON used 392 journal articles taken from earlier index language test. Each section gives a detailed descriptions of the index systems, of the results, of the expectations and the conclusions. The overall conclusions are clear: the most important factor in index performance in this test turns out to be index term context (the more the better), function words and term order do not matter as much. (KK)

#258(#256)   **[Review of] On the performance of nine printed subject index entry types** / Jutta Sorensen – *Journal of Information Science* (ISSN 0165-5515), 1(5)January 1980, p.303-305.

In EPSILON particular attention was paid to three design variables: (1) the provision of context; (2) the use of functional adjuncts; and (3) the order of index terms. These variables are not only related to entry-types investigated but also associated with particular 'live' indexing systems such as: Lead term alone (keywords without context), Rotated string (KWIC and KWOC), Articulated prepositional (ASI), Shunted relational (PRECIS) and Chain procedure (BTI). Points out that the documents used in EPSILON project were indexed only once, and that each original string was doctored in various ways to simulate other systems. Argues that different inputs would lead to significantly different outputs. EPSILON did not provide totally rigorous control of entry variables, nor did it allow each system to extent the maximum influence and difference that it could. Emphasizes that the findings summarized in the report cannot be related to 'live' indexing systems. Accordingly the author's assertion that some systems are " ... of particular operational interest" cannot be justified. (KK)

70 EVENTS FOLLOWING THE RESIGNATION OF THE FIRST EDITOR

After computerization of BTI, which brought the author index to BTI in 1972, Coates decided to accept an invitation to join the Working Group of the FID/SRC (Subject-field Reference Code), which was formed in the framework of the UNISIST programme, in 1973. He was elected one of the three-man panel of the new BSO (Broad System of Ordering) in September 1974, and became the second Rapporteur of the FID/BSO Panel in September 1977. In between, owing to his distinguished contribution, the 1st draft of BSO was completed in March 1976, and the 2nd revised (penultimate) draft in June 1977. The BSO 3rd revision was jointly published by FID and UNESCO in 1978. Cf. *BSO – Broad System of Ordering: an international bibliography* / comp. Keiichi Kawamura – Tucson, AZ, University of Arizona Campus Repository, 2011, 102p.

#259 **Publications. Serial publications [Mr Coates resigns from BTI]** – *Annual report of the Council of the Association for the year ending 31st December, 1976: Presented at the annual meeting in London 1977* – London, Library Association, [1977], p.20.

Mr Eric Coates, editor of *British Technology Index* since its inception in 1962, intimated his decision to retire in the Spring of 1977 and Mr Tom Edwards, editor of *LISA*, was appointed to succeed him. Accordingly, Mr Jeremy Digger, formerly Senior Research Assistant, Subject Systems Office in the British Library, was appointed to succeed Mr Edwards and he took up his duties with *LISA* in September. (Excerpt from original text)

#260 **New Editor for BTI** – *Library Association Record* (ISSN 0024-2195), 78(6)June 1976, p.285.

Tom Edwards, Editor of Library and Information Science Abstracts for the last eight years, has been appointed to succeed Eric Coates as Editor of British Technology Index. Mr Coates retires after 14 [sic] years as BTI's first Editor. (Original text)

#261 **Publications. Serial publications [Mr Coates resigned from BTI]** – *Annual report of the Council of the Association, for the year ending 31 December 1977: Presented at the annual meeting in Brighton 1978* – London, Library Association, [1978], p.11.

Mr Eric Coates retired from the editorship of *British Technology Index* in April and was replaced by Mr Tom Edwards. It says a great deal for them both that the changeover – a complicated operation – was effected as smoothly as it was. (Original text)

#262   **Publications. Serial publications [Subscriptions to the LA's periodicals]** – *Annual report of the Council of the Association, for the year ending 31 December 1977: Presented at the annual meeting in Brighton 1978* – London, Library Association, [1978], p.11.

Subscriptions to The Association's six periodicals continue to give cause for modest satisfaction, bearing in mind the difficult economic climate at present. While there has been a small drop in sales of *BTI* and *LISA* of about 50 copies each, all our other journals have maintained their sales and it is pleasing to be able to report that the *Journal of Librarianship* and *RADIALS Bulletin* both show satisfactory increases of over 5% and 10% respectively. (Original text)

#263   **[BTI part-time indexer]** – *Library Association Record* (ISSN 0024-2195), 80(1) January 1978, p.7. See also #269.

Martin Rowat has joined the staff of *British Technology Index* as a part-time indexer. (Excerpt from original text)

#264   **BTI survey** – *Library Association Record* (ISSN 0024-2195), 80(6)June 1978, p.275.

A Working party to examine prospects for the *BTI* was established by Council at the beginning of the year. The Chairman is Don Mason (CLW). At its last meeting, held on 12 May, editor Tom Edwards was asked to carry out a survey of users' opinion on certain aspects of the indexing system. Arrangements are now in hand and it is hoped to include survey forms within either the May or the June issue of *BTI*. Interested users are urged to help the Working party by returning their forms as soon as possible. (Original text)

#265   **Publishing. Serials and journals [Report of BTI survey]** – *Annual report of the Council of the Association, for the year ended 31 December 1978: To be presented at the annual meeting in Nottingham 1979* – London, Library Association, [1979], p.11. See also #252 and #268.

BTI subscriptions have remained constant. A working party was established at the beginning of 1978 to examine the prospects for the serial. Three meetings were held, and we conducted a survey of user opinion. Replies showed that users were satisfied with the service and, in particular, wanted the present method of indexing to continue. The working party's final report was accepted by Council in late 1978. Recommendations covered the establishment of an additional indexing post, the provision of a single-sequence authority file and the abandonment of the double entry system for the whole-part indexing situation. In December 1978 the BTI editorial office moved to Ridgmount Street, bringing the whole of the publishing operation under one roof. (Excerpt from original text)

#266   70 EVENTS FOLLOWING THE RESIGNATION OF THE FIRST EDITOR   #270

#266   **BTI moves** – *Library Association Record* (ISSN 0024-2195), 80(12)December 1978, p.649.

The editorial offices of British Technology Index are moving to 7 Ridgmount Street on the weekend of 16-17 December. Since 1962 they have been in the Euston Road and this move brings all the staff under one roof for the first time. (Original text)

#267   **BTI has moved** – *Library Association Record* (ISSN 0024-2195), 81(2)February 1979, p.91.

The editorial offices of *British Technology Index* have moved to 7 Ridgmount Street. Since 1962 they have been in the Euston Road and this move brings all the staff under one roof for the first time. (Original text)

#268   **Change in indexing policy [Foreword]** / T. Edwards – *British Technology Index* (ISSN 0007-1889), 18(1)January 1979, no pagination. See also #108 and #265.

New editor announces that during 1978 a small Working Party was set up by the Library Association's Council to consider various aspects of BTI. Part of its remit covered the indexing system, and a survey of users' opinion was carried out on this aspect. Analysis of the replies showed that a large majority of users were in favour of continuing with the present method of indexing. The Working Party decided that no radical changes should be recommended in this area, but there was a commendation that double entries for the Whole-Part relation should be abandoned. This recommendation was accepted by the LA Council in October 1978 and the new policy will take effect from this issue. Up to 1978 a double entry has been made in such situations as: (1) POWER STATIONS : Boilers, Oil fired and (2) BOILERS (Power stations) Oil fired. The second entry for the Part-Whole relation is now replaced by a single reference: (3) BOILERS, Oil fired : Power stations. See POWER STATIONS : Boilers, Oil fired. (KK)

#269   **Development of LISA and BTI [each increased by one indexer]** – *Library Association Record* (ISSN 0024-2195), 81(3)March 1979, p.110-111 (esp. p.110). See also #263.

The two serials, *Library and Information Science Abstracts* and *British Technology Index*, provide a large proportion of publishing income and their continued growth and strength are of high priority. To achieve these ends, the Council agreed last year that the staff for each serial should be increased by one indexer. Interviews are now being held for these posts and we hope the new appointees will take up their positions as soon as possible. (Excerpt from original text)

#270   **President and Fellows** – *Library Association Record* (ISSN 0024-2195), 81(7)July 1979, p.314.

Professor Wilfrid Saunders, Director of the Post-graduate School of Librarianship and

Information Science, University of Sheffield, was adopted as President-elect for 1980. Honorary Fellows elected were Richard Buchanan, Hon President of the Scottish Library Association and former MP for Glasgow, Springburn; Eric Coates, former Editor of *British technology index*; Bob Hilliard, former LA Secretary; Don Richnell, Director General of the Reference Division of the British Library; and Past President James Wilkie. (Original text)

#271 **Honorary Fellows** – *Library Association Record* (ISSN 0024-2195), 81(11) November 1979, p.514.

Five new Honorary Fellows were presented with their certificates at the Presidential session of the Nottingham conference: Richard Buchanan, Eric Coates, Bob Hilliard, Don Richnell and James Wilkie. All were presented to the meeting by Douglas Foskett, President in 1976. Foskett spoke about Coates that when BNB was started Jim Wells had recruited a formidable team, including Eric Coates. He was given the chance to put into practice his ideas, particularly on subject indexing. Later, when LA started the *British Technology Index*, though there had been previous efforts at indexing science and technology, all of which had failed, Coates had taken on this work and made it successful. (KK)

#272 **[Computer costs]** – *Library Association Record* (ISSN 0024-2195), 83(6)June 1981, p.307.

It is reported that the income from BTI subscribers in 1980 was £165,177. The expenditure on computer costs for BTI in 1980 was £7,150, which was 2.81 times as much as that of £2,544 for BTI in 1979 (*Library Association Record*, 82(6)June 1980, p.291). (KK)

#273 **Publishing Division. Serials [Changes in BTI]** – *Annual report of the Council of the Association for the year ended 31 December 1980: To be presented at the annual meeting in Margate 1981* – London, Library Association, [1981], p.20. See also #278.

British Technology Index appears in a new guise in 1981 as Current Technology Index (CTI). A large sum has invested in a completely new, specially written computer program, the abstruse parts of the content have been rendered more accessible and the whole book of the product is modern. Council approved the change of title in May for the clear reason that the new title reflects the major advantage of the product – that the currency of its entries is unmatched in any printed index: as little as 3 weeks may elapse between appearance in a primary journal and its appearance in CTI. (Original text)

#274 **New title for BTI** – *Library Association Record* (ISSN 0024-2195), 82(8)August 1980, p.353.

At the last Council meeting, endorsement was given to the Division's view that the title of BTI should be changed, to *Current technology index*, in 1981. This change reflects, on the one hand a great selling point of CTI, which is that it is the most current printed index on technology in the world (an article can be indexed and in print in CTI within three weeks of original appearance). Furthermore the previous title was misleading in that it implied that the technology was British. The coverage of subject content is, of course, world wide: it is the journals covered which are British. The new title, in January 1981, will coincide with a somewhat simplified indexing system and a clear new page layout. We believe users, particularly if they are not information specialists, will find CTI quicker and easier to use. (Original text)

#275(#274) **Perturbed at BTI change** / L.L. Ardern – *Library Association Record* (ISSN 0024-2195), 82(10)October 1980, p.487. See also #124.

I am perturbed at the note in "News from the Secretariat" (*Record, August*, p.353), that *BTI* will become *CTI*. As a member of Council 20 years ago, I helped John Bryon to bring his ideas for *BTI* to fruition and we gave a lot of thought to the title. The argument that British implies only British technology is nonsense. *British plastics* does not only deal with UK experience and there are many other similar journals. If the Publishing Division must have "Current", then print it as part of a descriptive sub-title, and do an article for the *New scientist* showing how current the index is (as we did for *BTI* in *Nature*, [218(5142)]18 May 1968 [p.623-624]). This would be more likely to bring in a few extra subscriptions and would not annoy a thousand (?) librarians who would have to alter their records to *CTI*. To suggest that only information scientists can **now** use *BTI* **easily** is an insult to the profession and to all information seekers. Lastly, *CTI* seems to offer more than we supply. It suggests a worldwide coverage. Let us continue to be honest! (Original text)

#276(#274) **"Founding fathers" were right** / E.J. Coates – *Library Association Record* (ISSN 0024-2195), 82(10)October 1980, p.489.

The author hopes to know more substantial reasons for changing the title of BTI than are offered in news carried in the August issue of the *Library Association Record*. Raises a question as to the CTI's great selling point of currency, and points out that the combination of currency with high indexing standards sell BTI. Doubts that an already profitable service can be made yet more profitable by a somewhat modified indexing system. Makes an objection to the LA's argument that the title of BTI misleadingly implies the subject matter to be British technology, and asks at what stage in marketing CTI will the prospect learn that CTI is limited to British source journals. Though the author was the first editor of BTI, he had no hand in thinking up the title. Feels that the founding fathers of BTI of 19 years ago displayed not only a proper sense of professional values, but also sound commercial acumen in going for a title. (KK)

#277 **CTI enters with a bang** – *Library Association Record* (ISSN 0024-2195), 83(3) March 1981, p.108. See also #281.

A NEW serial title has exploded upon the eye, thanks to LA Publishing. Vol 1, No 1 of

CTI replaced *British Technology Index* in January and the current in the new title is at least electric to judge by the arresting front cover. Apart from expanding coverage and acknowledgement of the international nature of the subject matter, *CTI* editor Tom Edwards operates with the same underlying principles of indexing and with the same format as *BTI*. Just to give a flavour of the subjects covered: eggs, minced beef and ice cream. (Original text)

#278 **Records of AGM – and *Record* on Council** – *Library Association Record* (ISSN 0024-2195), 83(10) October 1981, p.471. See also #273.

This is a partial report of the LA's annual general meeting (AGM) held in Margate 1981. Describes that L.L. Ardern (retired) complained of the "retrograde" renaming of *British Technology Index* as *Current Technology Index*. He claimed that it was misleading through failure to cover US journals. Alan White (Chairman of the General Purposes Committee) agreed that there had been two or three comments from members on the change but that this was really a matter for the Board of the Company. Also, Geoffrey Smith raised the problem of inadequacy of the reporting of LA Council meetings in the *Library Association Record* in discussion of the *Annual report*. (KK)

#279 (#265, #273 to #278) **Curiouser and curiouser** / L.L. Ardern – *New Library World* (ISSN 0307-4803), 82(978) December 1981, p.222-223.

States that the author does support Geoffrey Smith's plea that the deliberations of the Council of the Library Association should be more fully recorded in the *Library Association Record*. Argues that the Council made unfortunate decision as to the change of the title of BTI to CTI (Current Technology Index). The decision ignored the 1978 working party's report that a survey of user opinion showed that they were satisfied with BTI and wanted the present method of indexing to continue. Raises the following questions: (1) Does the title of BTI imply that the subject matter covered is British technology? (2) Has the CTI's new page layout been acknowledged by users? (3) Do users agree to the increased price of CTI while its content has been reduced owing to the new page layout? (4) Are users asked again these changes? (5) Did the publishing division ask the first editor of BTI, i.e. Eric Coates, a man with world-wide reputation, to comment on the proposed alterations? (6) Have they asked two or three of that publications committee of LA, including J.F.W. Bryon, which promoted the original idea of BTI 20 years ago? Concludes that the author would still like to know a reaction of the 1978 working party who made a positive report of BTI. (KK)

#280 (#279) **Tribute to Lawrie Ardern** / E.J. Coates – *Library Association Record* (ISSN 0024-2195), 88(12) December 1986, p.584.

The author first encountered Lawrence Leigh Ardern (1912-86) in 1961 in connection with *BTI* in its prenatal stage. At that time Ardern was a major driving force within the working party set up by the Library Association to investigate the feasibility of *BTI*. Emphasizes that without his determination and pertinacity in outfacing and overcoming obstacles, there would have been no *BTI* (and no *CTI* today). Later he was a great support and source of strength to the *BTI* staff. While the author was Editor of *BTI*, Ardern was an unfailing friend in need, admonisher, and always down-to-earth counsellor. (KK)

80 APPLICATIONS OF BTI SYSTEM INCLUDING TRIALS AND DISCUSSIONS

See also #169 and #180.

80.10 CTI

See also #28 and #29, each of which includes a description of CTI.

#281 **Current Technology Index (CTI). Vol.1, No.1** / ed. Tom Edwards – London, Library Association Publishing, January 1981-. Monthly and annual cumulation. (ISSN 0260-6593). See also #277.
   W.A.G. Alison, Chairman of the Board of Directors, LA Publishing Ltd., contributed a 'Foreword' to this first issue. The next two-page 'Introduction' by Editor of CTI gave an account of difference in indexing between CTI and BTI. (KK)

#282 **Foreword by the Chairman, LA Publishing Ltd.** / W.A.G. Alison – *Current Technology Index* (ISSN 0260-6593), 1(1)January 1981, no pagination. Reprinted as "**Introductory note by the Chairman, LA Publishing**" in: *Current Technology Index. Annual volume 1981* / ed. Tom Edwards – London, Library Association Publishing, 1982, no pagination. (ISBN 0-85365-875-7). See also #312.
   Describes that the LA has a long tradition of indexing and abstracting for 60 years. Great courage was shown in commencing these activities often in the face of difficult economic circumstances. CTI's predecessor, *British Technology Index* (BTI), was launched after the failure of two earlier commercial attempts at technical indexing. To the immense credit of Eric Coates and his various teams of indexers of *BTI* provided a professionally successful service for 20 years. Some have asked why it was necessary to change *BTI* in the financial climate of 1981. The printed page must look more attractive to the user. Emphasizes that a re-alignment of LA Publishing's approach to technical indexing was vital in an age of on-line searching. Efforts should be made to select indexing terms that are of demonstrable value to the searcher rather than an all-embracing approach with a surfeit of references. (KK)

#283 **Introduction** / Tom Edwards – *Current Technology Index* (ISSN 0260-6593), 1(1) January 1981, no pagination.
   Introduction to the first issue of CTI gave an account of difference in indexing between

CTI and BTI. It covers: journal coverage; indexing principles and changing areas; a modified system of inversion cross-references; terminology; page layout; and filing order. It also refers to the *Catchword and Trade Name Index* (CATNI) which will be published quarterly from March 1981 as a supplement to CTI. (KK)

#284 **Journal coverage** – *Current Technology Index* (ISSN 0260-6593), 1(2) February 1981, no pagination.

CTI will include all the journals on the BTI's list and during 1981 will extend coverage to include additional titles. Coverage of a few additional titles has already begun. A list of further 19 titles is given. These titles will be added to the list as issues are received in the CTI office. Consideration is being given to the further development of CTI. Various suggestions have been made, such as: (1) to include English-language periodicals published outside UK; (2) to cover the more "popular" journals, i.e. those available at newsstands as well as in libraries and information centres; (3) to index feature-style articles in newspapers; and (4) to extend coverage of the existing journal list to the articles and news items consisting of less than a page. (KK)

#285 **Catchword and Trade Name Index (CATNI). Vol.1, No.1** / ed. Tom Edwards – London, Library Association Publishing, March 1981-. Quarterly. (ISSN 0261-0191). See also class 20.70 Use of magnetic tape.

CATNI was a quarterly supplement to, and byproduct of, CTI whose magnetic tape was utilized. It was an index of firms' names, product names, and catchword and jargon with full bibliographic details appearing under each subject heading. Commencing with the March 1982 issue, CATNI also included the names of all vehicles indexed under their manufacturers. CATNI was published March, June, September and December. The December issue is a cumulative volume covering the whole year, i.e. it contains all the entries made in the first three issues of the year as well as new entries covering the October to December period. (KK)

#286(#281, #285) **[Review of] Current Technology Index [and] Catchword and Trade Name Index** / K.G.B. Bakewell – *Indexer* (ISSN 0019-4131), 13(2) October 1982, p.137-138.

The reviewer emphasizes that he must have provided a much less satisfactory service without the *British Technology Index* (BTI) which was first published in 1962. Now BTI has gone. Points out that the title of the *Current Technology Index* (CTI) is possibly misleading. Not all current technology is British, but the index is still restricted to British journals. BTI was systematic and specific. The unique indexing system was developed by the genius of subject index, Eric Coates. The indexing principles remain the same in CTI, but the structure of 'See' and 'See also' references has been changed mainly for the purpose of saving space. The 'Related headings' system continues to be used as in BTI.

Says that it may take a little time for people who have been used to the BTI strings to get used to the CTI system, but they should find that the advantage of specific indexing is still there. CATNI is a new supplement to CTI that is indexing CTI articles under catchwords and jargon, product names, and names of firms and other organizations. Each CATNI entry provides full bibliographic information, but its usefulness is diminished by a selective indexing policy. Concludes that CTI and its spin-off, CATNI, would seem to be worthy successors to BTI. (KK)

80.20 ASSIA

#287 **Applied Social Sciences Index and Abstracts (ASSIA)** / Peter Broxis – *Library Association Record* (ISSN 0024-2195), 88(8)August 1986, p.357.

The article consists of two parts: "An introduction" by the Library Association (LA) and "ASSIA" by Peter Broxis. In January 1986 the Board of LA Publishing Ltd approved the launch of ASSIA. Emphasizes that LA has not embarked on such a massive project since the launch of the *British Technology Index* (BTI) in 1962 (now *Current Technology Index* or CTI). The editor Peter Broxis, who has worked for BTI since 1965 and advanced to Chief Indexer in 1977, gives the background to this new venture. He goes on to say that the general layout of ASSIA will be similar to that of CTI, but that there will be some modifications to meet the particular needs of social sciences and to establish ASSIA's identity. Modifications include: (1) a somewhat different filing sequence; (2) a different typeface; and (3) the addition of an abstract. The combination of an indexing and abstracting sequence is a novel feature of ASSIA. The informative abstract should be up to 150 words and not repeating information given in the subject heading. Explains the reason for the high proportion of overseas journals chosen for abstracting. ASSIA will be published bimonthly and cumulate annually. The first issue will appear at the end of March or early in April 1987. (KK)

#288 **Applied Social Sciences Index and Abstracts (ASSIA). Vol.1, No.1** / ed. P.F. Broxis – London, Library Association Publishing, February 1987-. 6 issues per year and annual cumulatiom. Annual subscription, £350 (cumulation only £297). (ISSN 0950-2238).

Below are reviews and Editor's expositions of ASSIA. (KK)

#289(#288) **[Review of] Applied Social Sciences Index and Abstracts (ASSIA)** / Tom Norton – *Indexer* (ISSN 0019-4131), 15(3)April 1987, p.187.

ASSIA is a new indexing and abstracting service launched in 1987 to cover social work and the whole range of personal social service, with particular emphasis on UK literature. ASSIA indexes over 500 English journals from 16 countries. 70% of the journals are included within 4 months, and remaining 30% within 6 months. The general layout is similar to that of the *Current Technology Index* and so is the indexing: it is a modified form of the chain indexing system developed by Eric Coates, with a reference from each step in the chain. Where necessary in ASSIA, terms are permuted to ensure that the user will get to the subject heading in one step in most cases. Each entry has an informative abstract (maximum of 150 words) and it is claimed that the combination of an indexing and abstracting sequence is novel and designed to make searching easier for the user. ASSIA also has an author index with the journal reference and the first two terms of the subject headings cited against each entry. (KK)

#290 (#288) **ASSIA – a daring and valuable professional venture [Review of]
Applied Social Sciences Index and Abstracts** / J.A. Foskett and D.J. Foskett – *Library Association Record* (ISSN 0024-2195), 89(11) November 1987, p.600-601.

Review of the first two issues of ASSIA. Over 500 periodicals are monitored by a team of 6 indexers at ASSIA. Editor of ASSIA, Peter Broxis, has long experience of working with Eric Coates at BTI, which has made him expert in all aspects of such work. The monthly issue consists of 3 sections: (1) list of periodicals indexed; (2) subject index and abstracts; and (3) author index. The main entries of the subject index contain: title, author, periodical citation, and informative abstract of up to 150 words. The author index consists of periodical citation and subject heading. The index element taken two main forms: "See" references and "Related headings." The form of heading for main entries and "See" references consists of detailed subject analysis based on facet principles. The facet terms are separated by a colon, e.g. 'PAIN : Surveys'. National and race adjectives follow their noun in brackets, e.g. 'UNIVERSITIES (Israel) : Students (Arabic)'. Adjectives indicating types and subclasses follow a comma, e.g. 'HOUSING, Rental'. Relation indication "and" is shown by a hyphen, e.g. 'MARXIST-FEMINIST PERSPECTIVES'. Points out 9 matters to be improved in. Recommends ASSIA to all librarians concerned with social problems. (KK)

#291 **ASSIA: a new reference work for the social sciences** / P.F. Broxis – *Serials* (ISSN 0953-0460), 1(1) March 1988, p.55-57.

The first editor of ASSIA says that he was for many years on the staff of BTI/CTI, and that ASSIA is designed to cater for the needs of those who are concerned with the issues affecting the lives of people in society including youth, ageing, ill health, handicap, and housing. Traces the background to the launch of the service in 1987. A novel feature of ASSIA is that the abstracts are not numbered but arranged under alphabetical subject headings. Another feature of ASSIA is its network of related headings which direct the user from general to more specific terms. Considers some of the lessons which have been learned in developing the service. (KK)

#292 **ASSIA: Applied Social Sciences Index and Abstracts – a new approach to social science information** / Peter F. Broxis – *International Forum on Information and Documentation* (ISSN 0304-9701), 14(1) January 1989, p.8-11.

Defines the subject scope of ASSIA and the key areas covered and describes the principles for material selection, the service structure, indexing techniques, and future development. ASSIA differs structurally from other abstracting services in that the entries are not numbered, and a single alphabetical sequence is possible combining bibliographical citations under the main subject headings, cross references and related headings. The terms within the subject heading are referenced back by a modified form of chain indexing, which was initially advocated by Ranganthan and modified by E.J. Coates for the *British National Bibliography* and later for the *British Technology Index*. Emphasizes that chain indexing has certain limitations, but it has the advantage of producing a consistent index economically. (KK)

#293 **ASSIA social science information service** / Peter F. Broxis – *Outlook on Research Libraries* (ISSN 0165-2818), 11(2) February 1989, p.3-8.

ASSIA started in 1987 as a bimonthly indexing and abstracting service in the field of sociology, and was aimed at practitioners as well as sociologists. Considers arrangement of ASSIA, journal coverage, indexing approach, services for subscribers, and who are the users? The indexing techniques used in ASSIA are designed to be simple and employ the methods of facet analysis and chain indexing. The latter was first developed by Ranganathan and later modified by E.J. Coates for the *British National Bibliography* and subsequently for the *British Technology Index* (now *Current Technology Index*). These techniques are both versatile and simple to apply, while yielding a consistency of practice across broad subject fields. (KK)

#294 **ASSIA: a valuable source of reference or an expensive and unwieldy irrelevancy?** / Victoria Fenerty – *New Library World* (ISSN 0307-4803), 91(3) March 1990, p.5-7.

Describes the aims and work of the Applied Social Sciences Index and Abstracts (ASSIA) as providing a clear path to information for most research questions in social sciences in a clear and user-friendly format. Discusses the chain indexing method and the use of CD-ROM. Chain indexing is originally evolved by Ranganathan and then modified by Eric Coates for use on the then *British Technology Index*. It contains a reference from each step in the chain. An index string consists of an ordered sequence of descriptors beginning with the key term of principal focus that is followed by parts or properties, actions, processes, agents, means, place and time. Concludes that ASSIA deserves the recognition and praise that reviewers have given it but that librarians have so far chosen to ignore it. (KK)

80.30 NRPRA

#295 **British Technology Index as a basis for the subject catalogue in the Natural Rubber Producers' Research Association** / G. St C. Cornwall, K.P. Jones and A.M.

Pattin – *Catalogue & Index* (ISSN 0008-7629), (12) October 1968, p.8-10. See also #158, #165 and #296.

The library of the Natural Rubber Producers' Research Association (NRPRA) was founded in 1938. It covers five main subject areas: physics, chemistry, biochemistry, engineering and rubber technology. The stock amounts to about 3,500 books and more than 20,000 reports in addition to extensive periodical holdings. The library adopted the principles of the *British Technology Index* (BTI) system because of its combination of alphabetic simplicity with a strong hierarchical structure. It took about 18 months for re-cataloguing of the stocks. A considerable number of subject headings could be lifted direct from BTI. The new catalogue consists of two sequences: (1) a combined author and title catalogue in alphabetical order; (2) an alphabetical Coates-style subject catalogue, with a main entry for each item and its cross-references. Some modifications to suit the library's special need are also introduced. (KK)

80.40 Metal Box Ltd.

See also #127.

#296 **British technology index-type indexes** / K.G.B. Bakewell – In his: *Classification and indexing practice* – London, Clive Bingley, 1978, p.152-154, and 168. (ISBN 0-85157-247-2). See also #295.

This part is a section of Chapter 7: The alphabetical subject approach; pre-coordinate. Following a concise description of the indexing principles of the *British Technology Index* (BTI), introduces two instances adopting the BTI system. One is the library of NRPRA and the other is the Metal Box Ltd. At the Metal Box Ltd., reports, pamphlets, patents and similar materials are arranged numerically. Subject retrieval is effected by a computer-stored subject list which is produced monthly with annual cumulations. The subject headings exemplify the faceted principles of the Colon Classification, which is used for the book stock of the library. There are 122 major terms and these are broken down into subheadings which are introduced by distinct punctuation marks, such as colon (:) separating facets and dash (-) qualifying by such characteristics as property or type. Points out that the system has an obvious affinity with the BTI system, and adds that Coates who is the then editor of BTI advised on its implementation. (KK)

80.50 SEA project

#297 **Computer handling of social science terms and their relationships** / E.J. Coates – In: *EUDISED: European Documentation and Information System for Education. Volume III, Technical studies* – Strasbourg, Council of Europe, Documentation Centre for Education in Europe, 1969, p.52-83. (ERIC report, ED 040 726).

At the request of the European Documentation and Information System for Education (Council of Europe), E.J. Coates indexed a sample of sociology of education literature taken from a copy of *Sociology of education abstracts* [SEA] using the basic principles followed in the *British technology index* but with modifications to meet the particular needs of the literature and which do not present themselves in the field of technology. (P.F. Broxis, for source, see #188)

The report consists of 3 parts: (I) The BTI indexing system; (II) Possible application of the BTI system to the field of educational sociology; and (III) Specimen index. Part I outlines the role of subject relationships in forming the base for both manual and computer versions of the concept indexing system used by BTI. There are 4 indexing processes: (1) summarization of a chosen document, which involves concept analysis; (2) vocabulary control using an authority file; (3) syntactic organization of index terms indicated by both the 'positional rules' and the relation indicating 'punctuation symbols,' and chain procedure for generating inversion cross-references from subject headings; and (4) hierarchical organization of index language leading to the names of related terms comprising species of the broad concept in the subject headings. Part II argues that while the same 4 indexing processes of (1) to (4) can be applied to any field, one particular subject field may demand more or less effort than others at any given point in the above processes. The difficulty in social sciences is an abundance of terms on the meaning of which is not even approximate agreement. Another different point is that the main category of concepts in social sciences is: Kinds of Human being, by age, sex, occupation, economic class, educational status, and so on. Two ways of coping with the difficulties are: (a) to cause meaning to depend upon 'position' in the string of terms; and (b) to indicate the active or passive role of the main category by 'punctuation symbols.' Part III demonstrates the possible application of a computer manipulable relation-based index structure, which is similar to that of BTI, to 108 document data extracted from the *Sociology of Education Abstracts*, 4(4)1968. Emphasizes that various rearrangements departing from the Specimen index are possible without impairing the integrity of the underlying system. (KK)

#298 Investigation into Sociology of Education Abstracts: Volume 1, Report on first stage of project / D.F. Swift, V.A. Winn and P. Jackson – Oxford, Oxford University, Department of Educational Studies, 1970, 276p. (OSTI report, 5074/1) (ERIC report, ED 054 780).

The OSTI-SEA (*Sociology of Education Abstracts*) project was conceived as a result of the awareness that the task of SEA as a service was steadily increasing in complexity and size. A three-year project was initiated to develop a system to meet information needs, patterns of inquiry and preferences as to type of service of its users. The study covered the selection process and present use of the literature, document description which dealt with SEA abstracts, and users and user needs. Suggestions are presented which represent a reasonable compromise between the "best" view of experts and the majority view. SEA is a service for specialists and although there is a feeling of obligation to meet the needs of a wider clientele, the service to specialists is of higher priority. (Original abstract)

From the viewpoint of applicability of indexing system to SEA, assesses three main systems developed in UK: (1) M.F. Lynch's *Articulated Subject Index* (ASI); (2) D. Austin's *PREserved Context Index System* (PRECIS); and (3) E.J. Coates' *British Technology Index* (BTI). As to BTI a sample of index has been independently produced by Coates (see the preceding entry). However, the report says that it is difficult on this base to examine the potential of a BTI-style system with regard to indexing the literature of SEA because of problems in terminology and concept analysis. The latter problem is concerned with the difference between a BTI-style system and SEA in relation to the extent of 'exhaustivity' and 'specificity'. (KK)

80.60 STIR project

#299 **An indexing and retrieval service for statistical sources: a progress report on the STIR project** / Geoffrey Hamilton – *State Librarian* (ISSN 0305-9189), 23(2)July 1975, p.20-22.

This is a preliminary report of the 'STatistics Indexing and Retrieval (STIR)' project that started in January 1973. The purpose of the project is to analyze problems faced by librarians and users in locating source of UK statistics and to consider solutions to the problems. The STIR system makes a database for a retrieval system and a printed index. Three computer-aided string input indexing systems are nominated: (1) *Articulated Subject Index* (ASI); (2) *British Technology Index* (BTI); and (3) *PREserved Context Index System* (PRECIS). ASI is rejected for its lack of detailed rules dealing with complex terms. Of the remaining two, PRECIS is chosen for the reason that "it may be regarded as a development of BTI." But PRECIS is also rejected because of its unmanageable physical size and complexity. Suggests free text input to the retrieval system, and recommends a KWOC-type printed index, using the title of a table as a context statement. Discussion follows as to user needs, system structure, request-answering procedure, and so on. For the final report, see the next entry. (KK)

#300 **An indexing and retrieval service for statistics users: design considerations for a computer-based system; second report on the STIR Project** / G.E. Hamilton and K.I. Smart – Loughborough, Loughborough University of Technology Library, May 1976, 136p. (LUT/LIB/R12) (ISBN 0-904641-01-5).

For a description of the 1st stage of the Project, see [LISA abstract] 74/2888. A STIR system for the indexing and retrieval of published sources of UK statistics is technically feasible. The system would use the ASSASSIN programs to provide: (1) a controlled keyword and context (KWAC) subject index, issued at least twice yearly in microform; (2) a reference retrieval service based on the free text searching of terms within statistical tables. Among the topics considered by the Project were: the needs and preferences of STIR's potential users; choice of index language for the manual index – Articulated subject indexing, the *British Technology Index* system, PRECIS, KWAC; an assessment of available 'off-the-peg' information retrieval systems; ASSASSIN; indexing and searching, with emphasis on the use of links or similar devices to avoid false drops; cost estimates. After 1 year's full operation the total cost of developing and running STIR would probably be less than £250,000. This is not unreasonable when one considers that the sum spent on gathering and processing government statistics may be as high as £50 million per annum. (LISA 76/3536)

As to the choice of index language, see abstract of the preceding entry. The final decision was not KWOC but KWIC index, which consists of an assigned term and the title of a table, i.e. a table caption. (KK)

80.70 Decentralized indexing in a centralized system using classification

#301 **Centralized and decentralized abstracting and indexing in the light of Czechoslovak experience** / Josef Voracek – In: *Library systems and information services: proceedings of the second Anglo-Czech Conference of Information Specialists, London, 1967* / ed. D.J. Foskett, A. de Reuck and H. Coblans – London, Crosby Lockwood, 1970, p.95-102. (SBN 258-96773-0).

Since 1954, the Technical Documentation Centre of the State Technical Library has indexed literature in science, technology and economics. Centralized processing of the abstract by UDC has meant that subject areas were classified too generally and required a further arrangement by an additional principle although this would violate the unity of the UDC classification. Indexing as carried out by the *Engineering Index* (EI) and the *British Technology Index* (BTI) is now considered the most successful method of arranging information. The advantage of BTI system lies in that it permits rapid orientation in retrospective searching, since the arrangement of the terms is alphabetical and the indexing language pays due respect to relations between Things on the one hand and their Properties, Actions and Parts on the other. Discusses peculiarities in the Czech language that prevent its use in dealing with foreign language material. (KK)

#302 **UDC as the medium for information retrieval in the automated network of university and research libraries** [In Finnish] **Yleinen kymmenluokitus tiedonhaun valineena tieteellisten kirjastojen atk-verkossa** / Vesa Kautto – *Signum* (ISSN 0355-0036), 12(6)1979, p.103-108.

UDC is the most common classification scheme used in Finnish university and research libraries. The scheme has several disadvantages for decentralised classification including alternative levels of classification and uneven updating. An additional disadvantage for Finland is that most foreign literature is classified by Dewey, not UDC. UDC is a major advantage in searching, but an information retrieval system should allow searching by subject terms, rather than class numbers. PRECIS terms are not very suitable translated into Finnish; *British Technology Index* terms would translate well. The Finnish automated information retrieval system of university and research libraries is modelled on the Swedish LIBRIS system. (LISA 80/1451)

80.80 Recommendation for the index form in standards

#303 **The British Standards Institution and its recommendations for indexes /** L.M. Harrod and Mary Piggott – *Indexer* (ISSN 0019-4131), 10(4) October 1977, p.186-191.

This is an address to a meeting of the Society of Indexers held on 11th January 1977. The address consisting of two parts was given by two members of the Committee on recommendations for indexes of the British Standards Institution (BSI). The Committee drew up the *Recommendations for the preparation of indexes to books, periodicals and other publications* (BS 3700: 1976). The first part by Harrod sets the background by describing BSI, how BS 3700 fits into its activities, publication of the *Recommendation* and its relation with BS 1749 *Alphabetical arrangement* (1951) which is soon to be considered for revision. The second part by Piggott discusses the provisions of the new standard under the sections: scope; coverage; choice and form of headings and subheadings; cross references; arrangement; presentation; and the index to the standard. With regard to 'the choice and form of headings and subheadings' in the second part, Piggott introduced a suggestion which did not appear in the earlier edition. Explained that in setting out headings and subheadings, instead of successive indentations, a conventionalized single-line entry using punctuation marks with assigned and consistent meanings, may be used as in an example borrowed from the *British Technology Index*. For instance, 'HEATIHG, Gas-fired : Equipment : Safety' is interpreted by the user as 'Safety of equipment used in gas-fired heating'. (KK)

#304 (#303) **Editorial** / Leonard Montague Harrod – *Indexer* (ISSN 0019-4131), 11(1) April 1978, p.1.

Editor of *The Indexer* describes that he had to hand in his resignation at very short notice owing to the private and urgent problem. He expresses his gratitude to E.J. Coates, who was formerly Editor of the *British Technology Index* and has lectured to the Society of Indexers and written articles for *The Indexer* on several occasions, for undertaking the Editor's duty. Adds that not only did Coates do this, but he has also seen the duties of M. Piggott who was Assistant Editor and was unable to perform them through an accident. Emphasizes that this important issue would have been deferred without Coates' generous help. (KK)

#305 (#304) **History of indexing societies part IV: 1978-82** / Hazel K. Bell – *Indexer*

(ISSN 0019-4131), 21(2)October 1998, p.70-72.

1978 was the Society of Indexers' 21st anniversary year, which was greatly celebrated. The April issue of *The Indexer* that year, vol.11, no.1, had a special anniversary logo on its cover. The issue announced Harrod's resignation as editor, after 14 years. The anniversary issue was edited by E.J. Coates, former editor of the *British Technology Index*. (KK)

90 REFERENCES MADE TO BTI IN CONNECTION WITH RANGANATHAN AND CRG

See also class 00.60 References made to Coates' theory of subject catalogues.

#306 **Classification in university libraries** / D.J. Foskett – *Library Association Record* (ISSN 0024-2195), 66(1)January 1964, p.36-37. See also #310.

Makes a comment on a view that the Classification Research Group (CRG) lacks practical thinking and realistic objectives. In order to deny this kind of view, enumerates some 'public' activities of CRG. Mentions that the first of the activities is close association with: the *British National Bibliography*, the *British Catalogue of Music*, the *British Technology Index*, the *British Education Index*, and the Aslib-Cranfield Research Project. (KK)

#307 **Information indication – the role of conventional theory** / R.K. Olding – *New Zealand Libraries* (ISSN 0028-8381), 32(3)June 1969, p.95-102.

Outlines the ideas and methods of Panizzi, Crestadoro, Kaiser, Richardson, Bliss, Hulme, Cutter, Ranganathan, Prevost and Holmstrom. As to the idea of specific entry, contrasts Cutter's specific multiple entry with Ranganathan's subject specification single entry. Illustrates the difference between the methods of Cutter and Ranganathan with examples from the *Applied Science and Technology Index* and the *British Technology Index*, the latter of which is regarded as an alphabetical variant of faceted classification. (KK)

#308 **The work of the British Classification Research Group** / T.D. Wilson – In: *Subject retrieval in the seventies: new directions* / ed. Hans H. Wellisch and Thomas D. Wilson – Westport, CT, Greenwood, 1972, p.62-71. (Contributions in librarianship and information science, 3) (ISBN 0-8371-6322-6).

In early years, activities were concentrated on: (1) the development of special classification schemes using Ranganathan's facet analysis; (2) the investigation of notational systems; (3) the analysis of relationships between concepts. In 1962, the Library Association studied the feasibility of a new general classification, and appointed the CRG as its agent. Work has subsequently been concentrated on: (1) determination of principles for the categorization of concepts; (2) the ordering of concepts within categories utilizing the theory of integrative levels; (3) investigation of relationships between concepts. Other activities are: the revision of the library science classification scheme, the development of the English Electric Thesaurofacet and the Intermediate Lexicon Project. The special systems produced by members of the Group have been applied to the *British Catalogue of Music* scheme, the *British Technology Index* and the library science scheme used by *Library and Information Science Abstracts*. (LISA 72/2059)

#309 **Library classification: one hundred years after Dewey** / David Batty – In: *Major classification systems: the Dewey centennial; papers presented at the Allerton Park Institute Number 21 held November 9-12, 1975, Allerton Park, Monticello, Illinois* / ed. Kathryn Luther Henderson – Urbana-Champaign, University of Illinois Graduate School of Library Science, 1976, p.1-16. (ISBN 0-87845-044-0).

In assessing what exists today in the area of classification, it is necessary to review what has happened since Dewey. The genius of Dewey's achievement is noted. Discusses the creation of UDC developed from Dewey, the problems of early indexers using natural language, the work of Bliss, the contribution of Ranganathan and the work of the Classification Research Group (CRG). The significance of the CRG's early work was to develop a simple model for faceted classification that acknowledged the principle of decreasing concreteness for the assembly of components without imposing a limiting categorization. This led to work on a general classification funded by NATO and carried out by Derek Austin and to the new indexing system of PRECIS. Refers to Coates' contribution in connection with the acknowledgement of decreasing concreteness. He founded the *British Technology Index* and used CRG principles to organize natural-language subject headings of considerable complexity. In one sense Coates was heir to Kaiser, but in another his work was close to the Ranganathan/CRG tradition. Coates' automatic construction of references relies on the assumption that the decreasing concreteness terms are logical steps in a chain. (KK)

#310 **Tribute to Bernard Palmer [1910-79]** / D.J. Foskett – *Library Association Record* (ISSN 0024-2195), 81(5)May 1979, p.258-259 (esp. p.259). See also #306.

Perhaps the work in which he took the greatest personal pleasure was in classification, which to his orderly mind represented a peak of professional ideas. He studied with Ranganathan while with the RAF [Royal Air Force] in India, was duly inspired by that great man, and did more than anyone else to popularize his work in Britain. He was a clear and fluent writer, and with A.J. Wells [1912-93] and others, founded the Classification Research Group, which still meets regularly and has been the dominant influence on the theory and practice of classification and indexing: the *BNB* and *BTI* are eloquent witnesses. (Excerpt from original text)

#311 **The United Kingdom contribution to subject cataloguing and classification since 1945** / Eric J. Hunter – *International Cataloguing* (ISSN 0047-0635), 16(3)July-

September 1987, p.31-34.

Reviews the contribution of Ranganathan (1892-1972); the work of the Classification Research Group (CRG); the development of PRECIS; research into indexing language performance; automatic indexing and classification; major events in the sphere of general classification schemes; and the publication of monographs on the subject approach. The first meeting of CRG was held in 1952, the original members of which were: Palmer, Wells, Vickery, Coates, Farradane, Foskett and Mills. In his *Subject catalogues*, Coates summarized succinctly previous approaches and put forward his own theories as to subject headings. He shortly put his theories into practice in the *British Technology Index* (*now Current Technology Index*). (KK)

#312 **Preface to 1988 reissue** / E.J. Coates – In his: *Subject catalogues: headings and structure*, reissued ed. – London, Library Association, 1988, no pagination. (ISBN 0-85365-678-9). See also #1 and #282.

The new eight-page preface followed the preface to the original edition. Describes that the book was targeted both at advanced students and at practising subject cataloguers who were seeking an underlying intellectual coherence of the theory and practice in subject cataloguing. Argues that the *British National Bibliography* (BNB) commenced in 1950 marked a decisive break with the intuitive craft. The ideas set out in the book were product of ten years' experience in applying Ranganathan's principles. But the book had also a two-fold purpose comprising a down-to-earth element and a higher-flying element, the latter of which was later concerned with the *British Technology Index* (BTI). The tide of mechanization caught up the author around 1964 in connection with BTI, and resulted in an operational computer system in 1968. Points out that many of the effects of mechanization have been negative from the view point of technical excellence and economic justification. One can recognize this only to survey many of the big bibliographic databases and their hosts, and also only to consider the fact that (1) the virtual demise of BNB as a systematic conspectus for browsing and comprehensive broad searching from 1971 onwards, (2) the dropping the BCM classification from the *British Catalogue of Music* (BCM), and (3) the changes in format and arrangement in the former BTI from 1981. (KK)

#313 **The Classification Research Group – then and now** / I.C. McIlwaine and Vanda Broughton – *Knowledge Organization* (ISSN 0943-7444), 27(4)2000, p.195-199.

Following a description of the genesis of the Classification Research Group (CRG), traces the works of CRG members and those of CRG as a group. Says that work on the new *Bliss Classification* (BC2) has dominated the CRG during the 1990s. BC2 embodies many of the principles developed by the CRG in the creation of special classification schemes and indexing systems during the 1960s and 1970s. Though BC2 covers all the knowledge fields, the principal focus of discussions has been on the sciences. In this respect Eric Coates has been the major player, drawing on his experience with the *British Technology Index*, and in the development of the *Broad System of Ordering*. His input has been central to Classes AY/B, General Science and Physics, and C Chemistry, and with the publication of Physics and the virtual completion of Chemistry, he is now working on the Technology class, which has been hanging fire awaiting the final structure of the pure science classes. (KK)

#314 **Indexing and the Classification Research Group** / Ia C. McIlwaine – *Indexer* (ISSN 0019-4131), 23(4)October 2003, p.204-208.

Outlines the origins and achievements of the Classification Research Group (CRG) over the past 50 years since its establishment in 1952. Traces the CRG's role in the development of indexing principles and techniques from chain indexing and facet analysis to relational indexing and PRECIS. Notes that the *British National Bibliography* (BNB) started in 1950 provided a pattern for the catalogues that were found in libraries throughout UK for the next 30 years, i.e. a classified catalogue accompanied by a subject index. The subject index was constructed in the form of a chain index promoted by Ranganathan. Coates wrote a book "*Subject catalogues*" in 1960 that remains a staple text. He solved the problems of generating specific headings for complex subjects and put his ideas into practice in 1962, i.e. the *British Technology Index* (BTI). Like BNB, BTI adopted chain procedure to generating cross-references. In 1968 BTI was computerized and a method for generating these cross-references was devised. (KK)

#315(#314) **Editorial** / John Noble – *Indexer* (ISSN 0019-4131), 23(4)October 2003, p.185-186 (esp. p.185).

'Indexing and the Classification Research Group' by Ia McIlwaine was a walk down memory lane for me. Ranganathan, chain indexing, BTI, faceted classification, PRECIS; while some students revelled in these technicalities, others were terrified by them. I was somewhere in between, but it was the grounding in such matters and subsequent cataloguing and reference work in an academic library that gave me the confidence to think I could become an indexer. (Excerpt from original text)

#316 **Professional education: some reflections** / Kevin McGarry – *Education for Information* (ISSN 0167-8329), 18(2-3)October 2000, p.105-113.

Traces the development of professional education for librarianship and information science from the late 1970s/early 1980s to the present. Gives special attention to some of the important milestones, including aspects of curriculum development and the emergence of acceptable theories. In the 1950s S.R. Ranganathan was the most cited in textbooks on classification and subject indexing theory. There is little doubt of his influence on the *British National Bibliography* and the *British Technology Index*, largely through the work of A. Wells and E.J. Coates. Ranganathan's own publications were forbidding in their cultivated mysticism and an unnecessarily idiosyncratic terminology. While his own classification scheme was found to be unworkable as an intelligent shelf ordering for the location and retrieval of books, his PMEST categories had a talismanic effect. Concludes that very few LIS teachers understood Ranganathan, and that they became fewer still as the years passed. (KK)

#317 **A long search for information** / Brian Vickery – Champaign, IL, Graduate School of Library and Information Science, University of Illinois at Urbana-Champaign, 2004, 33p. (esp. p.12-13). (Occasional papers, 213) (ISBN 0-87845-123-4). Reprinted in: *Facets of knowledge organization: Proceedings of the ISKO UK Second Biennial Conference, 4th-5th July 2011, London* / ed. Alan Gilchrist and Judi Vernau – Bingley, Emerald, 2012, p.145-174 (esp. p.154-155). (ISBN 978-1-78052-614-0).

The personal memoir includes a statement of six figures out of the people who participated in discussions mainly at CRG meetings during the 1950s. The six figures referred to are: S.R. Ranganathan, Douglas Foskett, Jack Mills, Eric Coates, Jason Farradane and Robert Fairthorne. With regard to Coates the following statement is made: "Eric Coates was working as a cataloguer and classifier at the then recently established *British National Bibliography*. Earnest, sometimes a little severe, transparently sincere and humane, Eric later became the first editor of the *British Technology Index* and wrote a book, *Subject Catalogues: headings and structure*, much influenced by facet ideas. He has also played a major part in constructing and testing the *Broad System of Ordering*, a high-level classification system." (KK)

#318 **Ranganathan and after: Coates' practice and theory** / Keiichi Kawamura – In: *Knowledge organization and the global information society: proceedings of the 8th International ISKO Conference, 13-16 July 2004, London, UK* / ed. Ia C. McIlwaine – Burzburg, Ergon Verlag, 2004, p.337-343. (Advances in knowledge organization, 9) (ISBN 3-8991-3357-9).

This paper studies the works of Eric Coates who put into practice and advanced Ranganathan's thought mainly through the *British National Bibliography* (BNB) as its Chief Subject Cataloguer, the *British Technology Index* (BTI) as its first Editor and the *Broad System of Ordering* (BSO) as its Rapporteur. Following a description of these three systems demonstrated are: (1) how his works are connected with each other; (2) why his achievements should be estimated by a global standard; and (3) which of his contributions will throw light on unsolved problems in knowledge organization. The conclusion is that the underlying conceptual coherence in the work of Coates should be highly regarded as the persistent survival of interest and concern about classification despite its marginalization. (KK)

Author Index

The index refers to item numbers. Only individuals are indexed.

Aitchison, Thomas Morton .... #249, 250
Alison, William A.G. .... #282
Ardern, Lawrence Leigh .... #63, 65, 275, 279
Arends, Tulio .... #103
Ashworth, Wilfred .... #76
Auger, Charles Peter .... #177
Austin, Derek .... #182

Baer, Karl A. .... #223
Baker, E. Alan .... #235
Bakewell, Kenneth Graham Bartlett .... #48, 56, 122, 158, 179, 185, 286, 296
Barry, Hugh D. .... #200
Batty, Charles David .... #239, 257, 309
Beer, Ralph N. .... #62
Bell, Hazel K. .... #152, 155, 226, 227, 305
Bottle, Robert T. .... #116
Boussion, Anne-Marie .... #85
Broughton, Vanda .... #313
Broxis, Peter Frederick .... #188, 287, 291, 292, 293
Bryon, John Frederick Walter .... #135
Burton, Robert E. .... #90
Butcher, S.J. .... #7

Campey, Lucille Helen .... #232, 233
Cayless, Colin Frederick .... #209
Cemach, Harry Paul .... #66
Clough, Eric Allen .... #117
Coates, Eric James .... #1, 5, 6, 67, 69, 71, 73, 75, 78, 104, 105, 106, 108, 112, 149,
                                154, 159, 160, 161, 162, 168, 171, 174, 178, 186, 191,
                                208, 215, 216, 220, 224, 225, 248, 276, 280, 297, 312
Coblans, Herbert .... #212
Cole, F.D. .... #210
Cornwall, G. St C. .... #295
Corrigan, Philip R.D. .... #169
Cowley, J. .... #244
Cox, *Sir* Harold Roxbee .... #127

115

Croghan, Antony .... #23

de Grolier, Eric. *See* Grolier, Eric de
de P. Roper, Vincent. *See* Roper, Vincent de P.
Dove, Jack .... #81
Dunkin, Paul Shaner .... #4

Edwards, Tom .... #268, 283
Eichman, Thomas Lee .... #35
Eyre, John J. .... #184

Fangmeyer, Hermann .... #190
Farradane, Jason .... #86
Fathom, Ferdinand .... #83
Fenerty, Victoria .... #294
Ferriday, Peter .... #180
Fielding, Derek .... #181
Fjallbrant, Nancy .... #246
Flint, Margaret M. .... #118
Flint, William R. .... #118
Foskett, Anthony Charles .... #3, 24, 25, 26, 27, 28, 29, 30, 33
Foskett, Douglas John .... #8, 229, 290, 306, 310
Foskett, Joy Ada .... #290

Gee, Ralph D. .... #183
Gilchrist, Alan .... #164
Gorman, Michael .... #150
Gould, Angela Mary (*See also* Hall, Angela Mary) .... #253
Grolier, Eric de .... #15, 219

Hall, Angela Mary (*See also* Gould, Angela Mary) .... #249, 250, 251, 252
Hamilton, Geoffrey Eric .... #299, 300
Harrison, Kenneth Cecil .... #9, 98
Harrod, Leonard Montague .... #303, 304
Hawkins, B. .... #115
Hindson, Richard .... #70
Hines, Theodore Christian .... #213
Holloway, A.H. .... #68
Houghton, Bernard .... #114
Humby, Michael J. .... #229

Hunter, Eric J. .... #311

Hutchins, William John .... #34

Jackson, P. .... #298

Jenks, George M. .... #31

Johnston, Barbara .... #99

Jones, Kevin P. .... #165, 166, 295

Kautto, Vesa .... #302

Kawamura, Keiichi .... #113, 163, 318

Keen, Edward Michael .... #255, 256

Kelley, B. .... #115

Kilgour, Frederick G. .... #217

Kimber, Richard T. .... #187

Kumar, T.V. Remesh .... #41

Lavelle, Katherine Hope .... #249

Lewis, Peter Ronald .... #72, 74, 77

McGarry, Kevin .... #316

McIlwaine, Ia Cecilie .... #313, 314

Mee, E. .... #115

Metcalfe, John Wallace .... #36, 37, 38, 173, 182a

Mills, Jack .... #175

Mowatt, Ian R.M. .... #123

Neill, Samuel D. .... #32

Nemeth, Zsofia .... #16

Nicholson, I. .... #208, 214

Noble, John .... #315

Norton, Tom .... #289

Olding, Raymond Knox .... #176, 307

Osorio, Nestor .... #247

Parameswaran, M. .... #41

Paton, William Bryce .... #59

Pattin, A.M. .... #295

Pearce, B.L. .... #245

Piggott, Mary .... #303

Plant, Marjorie .... #10
Pohlman, L. Dawn .... #87

Rajan, T.N. .... #167
Ranganathan, Shiyali Ramamrita .... #172
Remesh Kumar, T.V. *See* Kumar, T.V. Remesh
Ritchie, Sheila .... #142
Roper, Vincent de P. .... #151
Rowland, Glyn .... # 114

Schwartz, Candy .... #239
Scott, P. .... #115
Sharp, Henry A. .... #11
Sharp, John R. .... #21, 79
Shimura, Hisao .... #40
Singleton, Alan .... #153
Singleton, William Thomas .... #89
Smart, Kenneth Ian .... #300
Soderland, Kenneth W. .... #12
Sorensen, Jutta .... #258
Spencer, Kenneth John .... #84
Supper, Reinhard .... #156
Svenonius, Elaine .... #19
Sweeney, Russell .... #39
Swift, Donald F. .... #298

Thornton, John Leonard .... #13
Thrash, James R. .... #88
Tomlinson, Norman .... #189
Trickey, Keith V. .... #18
Tynell, Lars .... #17

Urquhart, Donald John .... #64

Vann, Sarah K. .... #14
Vassilion, Epsevia .... #218
Vickery, Brian Campbell .... #157, 317
Voracek, Josef .... #301

Walford, Albert John .... #109

Weintraub, D. Kathryn .... #254
Wilson, Patrick .... #22
Wilson, Thomas D. .... #308
Winn, Viola A. .... #298
Wood, Charles Geoffrey .... #102
Wood, Neville .... #20

Language Index

The index refers to numbers of those items which are written in the languages concerned. Texts written in English are excluded.

Finnish .... #302
French .... #15, 85, 219
German .... #156
Hungarian .... #16
Japanese .... #40, 113, 163
Spanish .... #103
Swedish .... #17

Appendix
Title list of Coates' BTI-related works arranged in chronological order

Item numbers correspond to those in the systematic arrangement. Letters and book reviews are excluded.

1960: Subject catalogues: headings and structure .... #1

1962: British Technology Index .... #104

" Monitoring current technical information with the British Technology Index .... #105

1963: Aims and methods of the British Technology Index .... #106

" Introduction [British Technology Index. Annual volume 1962] .... #108

1964: Chain procedure: application in the British Technology Index .... #171

1965: Bibliographical indexes .... #186

1966: Scientific and technical indexing .... #149

1967: Control of vocabulary in a current awareness service .... #168

" British Technology Index – a study of the application of computer processing
to index production [with I. Nicholson] .... #208

1968: Report on 1st six months' production operational use of computer assembly of
cross reference data and compilation of authority file .... #215

" The computerisation of the British Technology Index .... #216

" Computerisation of British Technology Index: man-machine collaboration in
the production of indexes .... #220

" Computer assistance in the production of BTI .... #224

1969: Computerised data processing for British Technology Index .... #225

" Computer handling of social science terms and their relationships .... #297

1970: British Technology Index .... #112

1973: Some properties of relationships in the structure of indexing languages .... #159

1974: A comment on "Technical indexing at BTI." .... #154

1976: Card indexes or printed pages – physical substrates in index evaluation .... #248

1978: Classification in information retrieval: the twenty years following Dorking .... #161

1986: Tribute to Lawrie Ardern .... #280

1988: The role of classification in information retrieval: action and thought in
the contribution of Brian Vickery .... #162

" Preface to 1988 reissue [Subject catalogues: headings and structure] .... #312

川村敬一（かわむら・けいいち）

1948　青森市に生まれる
1972　神奈川大学経済学部卒業
1976　図書館短期大学別科修了
職歴　前獨協医科大学
　　　大正大学司書講習講師，淑徳大学兼任講師，英国 BSO 委員会編集顧問などを兼任
学位　博士（創造都市）大阪市立大学
著書　『BSO, あるいはCRGの新一般分類表－仮説と論証』博士論文，2013
　　　『情報資源組織演習』（分担）樹村房，2013
　　　『BSO - Broad System of Ordering: an international bibliography』University of Arizona, 2011
　　　「Ranganathan and after: Coates' practice and theory」『Advances in knowledge organization, 9』2004
　　　『サブジェクト・インディケーション』日外アソシエーツ , 1988 ほか

Bibliography of
the British Technology Index

2015年 8 月31日　初版第 1 刷発行

検印廃止　　　　著　者　川　村　敬　一
　　　　　　　　発 行 者　大　塚　栄　一

　　　　　　　　発 行 所　株式会社 樹村房
　　　　　　　　〒112-0002
　　　　　　　　東京都文京区小石川5丁目11番7号
　　　　　　　　電 話　東京03-3868-7321
　　　　　　　　FAX　東京03-6801-5202
　　　　　　　　http://www.jusonbo.co.jp/
　　　　　　　　振替口座　00190-3-93169

　　　　　　組版・デザイン／BERTH Office
　　　　　　印刷・製本／倉敷印刷株式会社

ISBN978-4-88367-250-9
乱丁・落丁本はお取り替えいたします。